New Earth – New Human
BE READY!

Stephanie Bunk

1. Edition, Feburary 2018

Title: New Earth- New Human – Be ready!
Author: Stephanie Bunk

ISBN 978-3-9819594-1-3

Book orders: www.new-earth-new-human.com

Proofreading: Francis Kundert

Cover design: Stephanie Bunk using an image of kevron2001, http://www.fotolia.de

Layout: Stephanie Bunk

Printing: BOD- Book on Demand
Printed in Germany.

© Stephanie Bunk
    E-Mail: siddhazentrum-markdorf@posteo.de

    Homepages: www.siddhazentrum-markdorf.de
                   www.maha-poorna-atma-yoga.com
                   www.earth-in-balance.org
                   www.new-energy-world.org

Contents

Chapter III
Prophecies for the coming time   56

Chapter VI

On December 10th, 2015, after the book was almost finished, I received the message from my spiritual teachers, Agastya Rishi and Lubamitra, who are guiding me since October 2013 through the palm-leaf-library, Jiva Nadi, that this work has been blessed and will spread worldwide. I would like to thank my beloved spiritual teachers with all my heart for their wonderful guidance and the great love with which they bless my life and that of others. This book is dedicated to them.

From which spiritual or religious tradition someone comes from is not important for this book. The message is universal. May God´s light, unconditional love and peace spread throughout the world.

Chapter 1
Way of realization

My inner journey started in 2009 with a prayer. In that prayer, I decided to dedicate my life completely to God and to follow his plan for my life. At this time, I couldn't even imagine what impact this prayer would have on my life in the following years. It was the beginning of an intense inner journey. I didn't know what kind of miracles were going to come.

STEPHANIE BUNK

My name is Stephanie Bunk. I was born in 1982 in Höxter, North Rhine-Westphalia. I studied Rehabilitation-Psychology at the University Magdeburg-Stendal in Stendal and worked as a family consultant for about four years for Caritas in Allgäu, Germany. Why I put a part of my biography in this place is intended to help the reader to understand that the realizations of this book are the result of an intensive and three years the long-term process of understanding. They were gradually revealed to me by the guidance of my spiritual teachers Agastya Rishi and Lubamitra.

Journey to Mexico

In 2011, I traveled to Mexico for the first time for about three weeks. We came with a group to work to strengthen the bridge between the spiritual Mexican traditions and Europe. During this time, a fundamental change took place in my life. During my journey, I felt I have to come back soon. Through clear inner images, I saw which places were waiting for me. After these intense weeks, I returned to Germany and left my old way of life in the coming months.

In 2012 I returned to Mexico. At that time I came for a year. From the beginning, I knew already that it would be an inner journey. I surrendered that journey to the divine guidance and traveled by following my intuition and the inner impulses I received. All the people I encountered at this time, all the places I visited were like a great gathering of an invisible force that conducted the event in a perfect and harmonious way, as in an orchestra. Sometimes I could not believe what was happening.

During this blessed time, I was able to participate in ceremonies of the Aztecs and Maya and to learn the Aztec dance in Mexico City. I traveled to Guatemala, attended a longer yoga retreat in the south of Mexico and lived for about three months with the Hare Krishnas. All these experiences were part of a training and preparation for what would follow in my life. I understood this only in retrospect.

In the last days of my trip, on 21.12.2012, I was led to a meeting. Shamans and healers from all over North and South America gathered in Cantona, a very ancient pyramid city in Mexico. Throughout the night, I sat with people from different nations and the elders of different traditions around the sacred fire. The elders talked about a coming new world.

In the morning at sunrise, we went up together to the pyramids to welcome the new time quality in a beautiful ceremony. At this time, I felt for the first time intensely that something very special is going to happen to the world. During this ceremony, suddenly a higher perception opened up, and I could feel something that I had never felt before. This feeling consisted of pure love, bliss, unity, light, peace, and harmony. After about two hours, the vision left me and a profound, unrecognized longing in my heart remained. I could not classify my experience at this time. I became aware of its significance and depth only three years later. I was able to feel the new time quality.

In February 2013 I returned from Mexico and rebuilt my life at Lake Constance in Germany. I moved into a beautiful community, got a job in a clinic and taught yoga at different places. Everything was as I always wished. But some part inside me knew ever since my return from Mexico, that my time in Germany would be of short duration.

A DECISIVE ENCOUNTER

In June 2013 I went to a lecture and met Sriraman for the first time. Sriraman comes from India and has been guided by Agastya Rishi through the Palm Leaf Library (Jiva Nadi) in India since he was 25.

THE PALM LEAF LIBRARY

The palm leaf library was founded by the Sapta Rishis about 7000 years ago. «Sapta» means «seven», «rishi» means «seer». They are considered to be direct students of Shiva. In the oldest Indian writings, Agastya, Bhrigu, Athri, and Vashishta are mentioned to be among the Sapta Rishis. A rishi is a seer who is able to receive absolute knowledge directly from the divine source and to teach it in its pure way. Absolute knowledge is characterized by the fact that it has universal validity and is timeless.

In total there should exist twelve official palm leaf libraries which are distributed throughout India. There are more in Sri Lanka and Bali. Also, there are private rooms, which keep individual palm leaves. The palm leaf library includes a large collection of palm leaves, which were described in parts over several hundred years, by the rishis. They are written in ancient Indian languages like «Tamil», «Sanskrit» and «Telugu». On the palm leaves are described the soul journeys of millions of people living today, as well as the history of mankind. The information comes from the Akashic record, an ethereal library where thoughts, words, and deeds of every human being are stored.

The purpose of the palm leaf library is to give companionship and guidance to those souls that come to visit one of the libraries during their lifetime. In a serious Nadi reading a person receives impressively accurate information about their past lives and how past life actions impact the present life. Furthermore, they also get information about how to harmonize their internal imbalances, to be able to create a happy and harmonious future.

There are two different types of palm leaf libraries. They are called Nadi Shastra and Jiva Nadi. The Nadi Shastra is similar to books that are already written and kept on a shelf, waiting patiently for their intended recipients to receive. They were already written down hundreds of years ago.

The other type, the Jiva Nadi («Jiva» means «alive») is like an online connection. Different spiritual masters like Agastya Rishi guide various people directly from the subtle world. The incoming messages relate to the current life situation of the led person. They are either received and written down in a channeling by a Nadi reader or appear spontaneously written by themselves by light on palm leaves. The information is then interpreted and transmitted by the palm leaf reader to the respective person, via telephone or through a personal meeting.

AGASTYA RISHI

Agastya Rishi is one of the founders of the palm leaf libraries and also the first Siddha of the master lineage of the 19 Siddhas. The 19th Siddha is Sri la Sri Mahananda Siddha. He lives about three hours' drive from Bangalore near Vellore. Since 2008, he is constructing a huge temple, which will be of great importance to mankind in the future.

The lineage of the 19 Siddhas comes from Tamil Nadu in South India. Tamil Nadu was part of the old «Kumari Kandam» (Lemuria). Kumari Kandam was a big country in the Indian sea. It disappeared few thousand years ago by a gigantic nature catastrophe. At that time man and nature lived for about thousands of years in their original natural state and in harmony with nature.

Agastya was, amongst other accomplishments, a great teacher of Ayurveda medicine, an alchemist and vedic astrologer. During his lifetime on earth, he was married to Lubamitra. Both work and lead today from the invisible subtle planes.

Sriraman is one of the closest disciples of Agastya. Since he aged 25 he is guided through the Jiva Nadi by Agastya Rishi.

After an intense period of two years traveling throughout India for fulfilling many tasks under the guidance of Agastya, Sriraman received a great blessing from Agastya. Whenever he will advise people, Agastya will stay in his consciousness to guide them, through Sriraman. Since that time, Sriraman is able to figure out by seeing the name and date of birth of a person, the potential of their soul, the internal imbalances that prevent him to express its power continuously and what instrumentality is needed to overcome that. Those who wish to learn more about the 19 Siddhas and the work of Sriraman are given detailed information in the brochure «The 19 Siddhas and Sriraman».

A LIFE-CHANGING DECISION

When I met Sriraman for the first time in this talk, I felt a completely undefinable feeling of being touched that came deep from my soul. On that day I felt intensely that I had encountered my spiritual teachers. Two days later I met Sriraman again in a consultation. Through the information, I received during this consultation my life changed again within a very short time. Sriraman said to me that I was ready for something, that I didn't understand at this time. He recommended me to come to India because something would wait there for me.

To be honest, I was not pleased about that news. I had other future plans at that time. To be able to listen completely to my inner, I deviated myself from all external influences for several days and went into an inner retreat. The deeper I went into my process the more I came back to the point where I clearly felt that it was my way to go to

India. Finally, after a long struggle, I decided to go. After three moves in one year, I left everything again and went back to India.

JOURNEY TO INDIA

When I met Sri La Sri Mahananda Siddha, the 19th Siddha, in August 2013 for the first time, I felt an indescribable feeling of meeting the Supreme Divine in person. I felt that the meeting with Sri la Sri Mahananda Siddha had been the reason for the last two challenging years and that all of my experiences before served as a kind of preparation.

The following time in India was full of blessings and challenges at the same time. I always had had doubts if my decision to go to India was the right thing to do.

In September 2013, Sriraman received a message from Agastya Rishi to travel with me to a certain temple. There I should light a pyramid with candles. Before I began, I prayed deeply to God. I asked him for a sign to show me clearly if I was on the right track and if what I was experiencing was really meant for my way. After all the lights were lit, suddenly a bright light went through my body. I could neither see nor hear for a short time. There were a loud inner rustle and a strong energy flow that streamed through me. Suddenly I fell to the ground. The priest of the temple interpreted this incident as a good sign.

The event was so intense that the doubts I had up to this time began to dissolve. First, the experience irritated me strongly. Afterwards, I knew that the impulse had been necessarily so intense that I began to believe.

AGASTY RISHI AND LUBAMITRA
COME INTO MY LIFE

In October 2013, I received the first messages from Agastya and Lubamitra through the palm leaf library. They told me that they wish to be my spiritual teachers, through Sriraman. At this time I didn't really know who Agastya and Lubamitra were. The knowledge came much later.

However, when the news of these two beings reached me, I felt like a child who had landed gently in the hands of the Divine after a long time of inner free fall. The invisible leadership, which I had already received and perceived in Mexico, was not an imagination. It was real and my spiritual guidance finally got a name.

Since that time, my path is guided through Agastya Rishi and Lubamitra by the spiritual subtle worlds. On the one hand, they lead me through written messages that enter the Jiva Nadi and on the other hand through inner inspiration.

During my time in India, I received many tasks from them which I had to fulfill. Among other things, in October 2013 I got the assignment to work for NEW ENERGY WORLD. The significance of NEW ENERGY WORLD for the earth and the people will be discussed in detail later in the book.

Return to Germany

In February 2014 I returned to Germany and opened in May the «Yoga und Siddhazentrum ZEITWANDEL» in Markdorf. This period in Germany was the most challenging time of my life. I had returned with these incredible experiences to the old world where I had to find my place again. I was also full of questions that would be answered much later. Sometimes I woke up in the morning, and it felt like all that I had experienced was like a great dream.

Babaji enters the Siddhacenter

In March 2014, before I opened the Yoga- and Siddha center, I visited a friend. I had visited him a few times before. But it was not until that day that I realized in a special way a picture of Haidakhan Babaji standing on an altar in his apartment. Haidakhan Babaji is considered to be a full incarnation of Shiva. He lived and taught in Haidakhan in North India and left his body on February 14th, 1984. Shiva is one of the many names for the Universal Divine Consciousness that incarnates at different times on Earth. It can adopt any physical form without having to go through the process of birth and death.

Before I learned about Haidakhan Babaji, I heard from Sriraman about Babaji Nagaraj. As I learned later, Babaji Nagaraj was a former incarnation of Haidakhan Babaji.

Babaji Nagaraj had appeared to Sriraman several years ago, in his subtle body. About five days he walked day and night through his living quarters giving blessings to Sriraman. Sriraman was so touched by his appearance that he did not dare to leave his house. Once during these five days, Babaji Nagaraj looked deeply into Sriraman's eyes. At that time Sriraman did not know who had appeared to him. Only a few months later he saw a movie about Babaji and recognized him.

On the day of my visit to the house of my friend something extraordinary happened. I asked him about the picture of Haidakhan Babaji. He told me about him. When he had to leave the room in between, he gave a CD cover to me on which Babaji was depicted. When I looked at it, suddenly Babaji began to speak internally with me. He told me that I should take him to my center. First I felt very irritated, but I asked my friend for a copy of the picture. In the moment he gave the copy to me, suddenly a strong blessing energy flowed through the room. First I thought that only I felt it. But when my friend turned his face to me, tears were also in his eyes. We both had felt it.

From the beginning of the opening of the center, Babaji´s picture was part of the Yoga and Siddha center. He showed me even where to place him. Throughout the year I kept asking myself again and again, what is the connection between the 19 Siddhas and Babaji?

ANY DOUBT WILL BE DELETED

In September 2014, I received the message from Agastya that the doubts that I had would be erased in the coming months. Up to this point, I have had phases in which I strongly questioned my experiences. A part of me could hardly believe what was happening in my life. On the one hand, the experiences seemed natural to me, but on the other hand, they were also strange. But one of their features was that from a certain point of my journey, they suddenly made sense and were important, for understanding the greater context, on a deeper level.

In December 2014, I led a satsang in the center. At the end of the event, a friend came to me. He told me that a similar meeting would take place near Markdorf on the following Sunday. He asked me if I would also like to join. In a meditation, I received the invitation to attend this meeting. So I went.

When I got there, I entered a very beautiful and powerful house. I felt like I was entering a temple and I was deeply touched by the perceptibly sacred atmosphere. The owner of the house and administrator of the place is a direct student of Haidakhan Babaji. Like other students, he had called her to Haidakhan through visions. On this day we performed a ceremony (puja) in honor of Shiva. I listened at that meeting to this message again: that the earth and humanity would soon enter a «Golden Age».

A NEW WORLD IS GOING TO COME

In the first week of January 2015, I was led by Agastya and Lubamitra through a deep process of realization, which lasted six days. All the information I received over the past year, came together into a growing picture. During these days, I completely lost my sense of time. Under the impression of my experiences, I began to realize that this new world would really come.

In this six-day process, an inner sentence came up in my inner and has not left me ever since: «Oh my brothers and sisters, there is not much time left!» Only a few months later I was able to understand the significance of this sentence. In context with that inner voice, an intense feeling arose that requested me to work hard and with great speed. This was also a message which I received constantly throughout the following year from Agastya and Lubamitra through the palm leaf library: «Work!»

After these realizations, I gave a talk in the Center. 28 people came in total. For the small Yoga and Siddha center, where a maximum of nine people can practice yoga, this was a considerable number and remained unique.

The next day I expected a friend's visit. She was not able to come to the talk the night before. So I decided to give a personal talk to her to share this information. Before I started, we came into conversation. Without telling her about the content of the lecture, she told me that she regularly follows a homepage of a Russian professor. That professor receives messages from the divine source about the current processes in nature and shares them on his website. My friend told me that this professor would say that a new world would come. She only told me, in other words, what the essence of my lecture had already been.

It was fascinating. Both of us had doubts if the information she and I had received were true. After I had given her the lecture, we were both impressed by the large overlaps.

The decisive event, that caused my inner doubts to finally dissolve, was a meeting with the director of a Yoga center in Germany. For a long time, I felt a strong inner impulse to meet him. It was April 2015 when I decided to drive to him. After I had made the decision, everything fell into its own place. I got a ride and was able to reorganize my center activities effortlessly. Before I drove to him I tried to get an appointment with him, which was not possible. Therefore, I made my way with confidence that if it was the desire of the Divine that we should meet, so it would come about.

When I was there, he made a few minutes available, for a conversation for the following morning. I was very grateful for it. In this conversation, we exchanged our experiences. Through his spiritual master, he had also learned that a new world would come.

SECOND JOURNEY TO INDIA

In August 2015, I went to India for another four weeks. During this time, further puzzle pieces were added to the overall picture. In India, I learned that, according to Sri La Sri Mahanandha Siddha, the 19th Siddha, the temple will become one of the most important places in the new world. I also was informed by Sriraman, that according to a message of Agastya, Sri La Sri Mahananda Siddha is Shiva personally, in physical form.

THE BLESSING

In July 2015, Sriraman received the message from Agastya Rishi that, in addition to him, further persons will be authorized to initiate people in Maha Poorna Atma Yoga. Maha Poorna Atma Yoga» means «great cleansing of the soul». It is a simple practice that cleans the unconsciousness of old impressions (samskaras) and frees

15

access to the soul's inner knowledge by reducing the energetic charge on destructive reaction patterns and emotions like fear, anger, jealousy, guilt, shame, etc.

Furthermore, Sriraman received the message that once the soul is initiated, the cleaning frequency of Maha Poorna Atma Yoga remains activated for several lives. Also, he was informed that the practice of Maha Poorna Atma Yoga will increase light in collective consciousness rapidly. Why this is of so much importance will become clear in the course of the book. On August 19, 2015, during my stay in India, I received the blessing from Agastya to initiate in Maha Poorna Atma Yoga.

The Earth will purify itself

After Agastya's authorization, I began to deepen the question why Maha Poorna Atma Yoga is coming to people at the present time. I felt, and already knew, that something gigantic is going to happen on earth, but I couldn't take it at that time. My internal question led me to a further process of realization in September 2015. I hoped to find an answer and started researching. In these days, I found out that several independent sources consistently spoke about a «cleansing process of the earth». This purification could be associated with great geographic upheavals and would introduce the new era on earth.

I asked Sriraman to ask Sri La Sri Mahananda Siddha if

this cleaning process would really come. Sriraman told me that Sri la Sri Mahananda Siddha had already announced this several times.

With this information, the picture became suddenly clear and complete. I understood the inner sentence, which had not let me go since January 2015. «Oh my brothers and sisters, there is not much time left!» I also understood the outstanding importance of the work of the 19 Siddhas and the importance of Maha Poorna Atma Yoga, NEW ENERGY WORLD, Agastya's work through Sriraman, and the importance of the temple that Sri La Sri Mahananda Siddha built.

May all humans awaken NOW, engage themselves and work together and selflessly for the good of the earth and of all mankind. The time available to initiate changes, that will avoid greater future consequences and challenges, is both urgent and limited. May this book awaken all of you and serve as a source of inspiration to you. **OM SHANTI!**

Chapter 2
The current processes
in nature

Nearly all spiritual traditions and religions around the world, but also many spiritually open-minded people, know that the earth and mankind will enter into a new era of time and that a great transformation process is currently happening in nature. This process is expected to accelerate towards a peak event. To give a better understanding of this, it is important to give some background knowledge.

CONSCIOUSNESS

Every human being and every living being is surrounded by an energy field which contains their complete energetic imprint. This imprint was planned by the soul itself before taking birth and is brought by being born, into the present life: mental and emotional strengths and weaknesses, life tasks, karma, vitality, the soul potential etc. All these aspects of our consciousness are connected to each other and interact. Together they create our reality and determine how we are looking at ourselves and the world.

Through experiences which we make during our lifetime, the energy imprint can be changed.

Our consciousness creates a powerful energy field that is comparable to a broadcasting station. We continually send out information in form of energy frequencies to our environment and receive them from other beings. The information exchange takes place within milliseconds and on a non-verbal energy level.

People who are empathic and live in the present can feel and correctly decode this non-verbal information immediately. In, general, it can be said, the more subtle the consciousness of a human being is and the more trained he is, the more clearly and precisely, he can perceive and interpret the energetic information he is receiving. The rougher the consciousness of a human and the more untrained he is, the more unclear and less differentially he perceives the transmitted information.

The energy field always speaks the truth, no matter if we are aware of it or not. The more we are connected to our soul, the more we learn to distinguish between the truth and untruth aspects within ourselves and in others.

SOUL-CONSCIOUSNESS VS. EGO-CONSCIOUSNESS

What is a soul? A soul is our true, authentic self or better expressed; the unconditioned self of human. It is the place inside us where we are present, creative, and free from reactive impressions and patterns. When we experience our soul we are connected with unconditional love, presence, neutrality, pure consciousness, universality, selflessness, harmony, creativity, inner peace and pure information. This consciousness is called «soul consciousness». It can also be expressed as «spiritual consciousness».

Through the soul, we are connected to a collective field of consciousness that interconnects all life. The soul allows us potentially to communicate with all living beings in nature through our intuition. This includes plants, trees, gemstones, animals and subtle beings. The degree of purity of our consciousness determines if and how we receive information from the divine nature.

In consumption orientated societies, people mainly live from the ego-consciousness. Therefore, many people perceive the light and knowledge of their souls only in a very limited way.

Shortly explained, the ego is a false and limited self-image that man has created for himself. It exists because of unknowing one's own divine nature. Because of this, a human identifies himself with character features, ideas, expectations, imaginations, thoughts, and feelings that come from the ego. He identifies himself with a false «I am» that covers the light of the soul. This veil is responsible for blocking access to our soul wisdom. In man, there arises a kind of self-centered parallel reality, which forms a limited reality. Depending on the extent of the ego, this veil is more or less strongly compacted and the perception is distorted.

Currently, many people are still in a deep sleep and do not remember their divine origin. There are many people who don´t even believe in the existence of their soul and in their own divinity. Inner impulses and spiritual experiences that come from the soul are considered to be a fabrication. The unconscious person doesn´t know that potentially he could access to a higher form of existence if he would engage himself in a process that is called «awakening». In this process, the consciousness of a human returns back to his own divinity.

PROCESS OF AWAKENING

When a person awakes, first she becomes aware of her selfish motives (shadows) and the old wounds that she is still carrying within. She begins to understand that they are the cause of her separation from the original source, and she starts to engage in a healing process.

Through this healing process, she gradually overcomes ignorance and disbelief and starts to experience a higher way of thinking and being. In this way, her trust in the existence of the soul grows and her connection to her inner divinity becomes stronger.

If a person starts to follow the impulses of the soul step by step, she is on the best way to bring her life back into

harmony with nature. The awakened human being has found a trustworthy inner leader and teacher in the soul, who shows the way in both the inner and outer life.

If we live in harmony with the soul, miracles in life begin to manifest. We get all information we need to be able to fulfill our destiny.

To support this process in a positive way, it is important that we support the purification of our consciousness. This helps the mind to calm down and to become more sensitive to the impulses of the soul and its guidance. Maha Poorna Atma Yoga, Hatha-Yoga, and Meditation are great helpers in this process.

CONSCIOUSNESS AND THE INDIVIDUAL

The consciousness of an individual always affects the individual and the collective consciousness at the same time. Everything is interconnected and influences each other. On the individual level, our consciousness affects, on one hand, what kind of experiences we make in the physical body, and on the other hand, what experiences we will experience after death.

First of all, it is important to understand that nature always says «YES» to our present state of consciousness. It doesn't matter if we are conscious or unconsciousness about the contents of our consciousness. This means for example, that a person, whose current inner attitude is determined by negativity, is more focusing on the negative aspects of her experiences and increases them through the law of resonance. A person who thinks optimistically and positive mainly sees the good aspects of her experiences and strengthens them. We always multiply and strengthen what we feed with our attentiveness and energy.

How a person evaluates her experiences is connected to her inner judging system, which is also formed by education and social norms. These imprints are called conditioning. Conditioning consists because of false beliefs, which don´t correspond to the divine truth. They are stored in the subconscious mind. They determine how something has to be seen and affect our consciousness and actions. Conditioning presents that a human connects with his creative and spontaneous original nature.

In soul consciousness, the human mind serves as a mediator between the soul and the external world. It is the instrument that helps to express and manifest the soul's creative impulses. The abilities of the mind are deliberately and purposefully used to realize the impulses of the soul and to manifest them in the external reality. Mind and soul work together harmoniously.

In ego-consciousness, the cooperation between mind and soul is disharmonic. The impressions of the conditioned subconscious mind suppress the impulses of the soul. The result is a mental field, which works self-willed and in a way that is contrary to that of the soul. The consequences of this way of life are detours and entanglements.

To be able to live in harmony with our soul and to perceive continuously her guidance, first, we have to purify our consciousness from old destructive emotions and thought patterns. They pull our consciousness into the past and distort the impulses of the soul. They can only be felt when we stay present.

Only when we live from the resonance field of our soul, do we activate the potential that is inside ourselves, and create circumstances in our lives which correspond with her powers. This leads to fulfillment and joy.

Until we reach this point, we will face experiences that relate to our ancient wounds and impressions. They help us to cleanse injured emotions, by neutralizing them and correcting false thought patterns, by bringing our thinking into harmony with the soul. Healed emotions and thoughts are characterized by positivity, harmony, peace, and love.

CONSCIOUSNESS AND AFTERLIFE EXPERIENCES

The consciousness of a person, as already mentioned, influences also, which experiences we face after our physical death. This is a very important point that only a few people think about during their lifetime. One of the reasons why they fear death is the fact that they avoid the transformational confrontation with their own transience during their lifetime.

Everyone has to die. This is certain to every human being from birth. If we run away from our mortality for a lifetime, we lose the chance to live a life of greater depth, gratitude, and awareness.

We should understand that death is nothing more than a transformation process into another form of existence. The experience that we have after our physical death depends on how we have lived our lives. And also, the state of consciousness in which we have left the body at the time of death. The law of resonance remains effective even after our physical death and will connect us with those experiences which correspond to the current state of development of the consciousness.

If we were not angels during our lifetime, we cannot expect that the heavenly realm will open up to us after our physical death. This is not a punishment. Our consciousness is simply not resonating to the heavenly realms.

For this reason, it is recommended to live a life in harmony with ethical values. This leads the mind into a harmonious state and will positively influence the experiences we make after our death. In this way, we can even influence our next incarnations in a positive way. At this point, I recommend the film "Astral city - Our Home", which depicts the worlds beyond, in a very vivid and touching way. We should learn about this issue to expand our perspective on life. There is a lot to win!

Consciousness and the Collective

The state of consciousness of a single human has a strong impact on the collective field of consciousness. It is co-creating the happenings on earth and in the cosmos. Our influence is bigger than we can imagine. In science, this effect is called the «butterfly effect». It describes that only the flapping of wings can be part of an impulse that creates an eventual storm from the soft to the powerful.

Looking back on the history of mankind, one can observe that just one human being can have a long-term influence on the world, either towards war or towards peace. Which kind of world we create depends on our decisions do we follow the impulses of the ego or the impulses of the soul?

Each person carries the responsibility for his own action and his own life. At the same time, he is also responsible for the happenings on the earth and for his fellows. If the basis of our consciousness is egoism, negativity, and selfishness, we create an environment of separation and destruction. Often we are not even aware of the subtle effects of our actions. An example will illustrate what is meant:

Peter and Reinhard are colleagues and work in the same department. Peter has a bad day. Like always it is already pre-programmed that someone will be attacked by his bad mood. His colleague Reinhard is just coming to the door. He will ask Peter for an advice, which he urgently needs to complete his project. For a few months,

Reinhard suffers severe depression and often thinks about committing suicide. He feels like a failure and rejected by the world. Quickly everything becomes too much for him.

When Reinhard enters the office of Peter, he already notices his rude look. Peter replies to Reinhard by only seeing him: «Don`t disturb me. I have no time for you. I have to work on my own stuff. »

On that day Peter's words are like a blow to Reinhard´s face. He feels incapable and once again confirmed that he is failing on all levels. The situation brings everything into the overflow. In the evening he sees no way out of his situation and hangs himself in the attic.

The tragedy of that story is realistic and is happening every day all over the world. How many jobs and schools are affected by mobbing? Many people are unaware of what they trigger through their careless behavior. The story is intended to illustrate the subtle significance that an ignorant and egoistic behavior, which many people show nowadays, can have.

Maybe a sincerely kind, supportive, and understanding word from his colleague Peter would have been enough on that day to give Reinhard hope and to dissuade him from his suicidal thoughts. Perhaps it would have helped him to overcome his acute crisis in a better way.

If we would consistently focus our consciousness on unconditional love, peace, understanding, positivity, kindness, and unity, we would have the power to transform everything around us into positivity and luminosity. If we would convert judgments into understanding and compassion, if we would be loving, mindful, kind, and gentle with ourselves and others, our life would return to color, joy, and luminosity. We would create a world that would be livable and loveable for us and other beings. This requires that we overcome ignorance and selfishness and make our light shine again.

In this simple way, everyone can do great things for improving the world. Once I read that a single human being who has attained enlightenment has such a strong energetic radiance that he is able to balance the imbalances of many thousands of unenlightened people together. That is tremendous.

Consciousness can Transform itself

The term «Veda» comes from Sanskrit and means «knowledge». The saints of the ancient times knew that humanity will enter into an age in which they will forget their divine origin. To ensure that the universal knowledge doesn´t have lost, they wrote it down more than 5000 years ago. As a result, the Vedic scriptures have arisen. The Vedas contain the complete wisdom of nature and its laws. They are timeless and universal. The knowledge was seen and received by Rishis (seers) and is the highest level of existing knowledge. It is timeless and universal.

In Vedic cosmology, fourteen levels of existence are described in total. According to the Vedas, each of the fourteen existential planes represents a planetary system that vibrates on its own consciousness frequency. Four of the fourteen existential planes belong to the luminous planetary systems. Three belong to the middle ones. The earth is part of this plane. Furthermore, it has seven underworlds, which are also described as hells.

Interestingly, this thrice divided cosmology is described in all spiritual and religious traditions. In Christianity and Islam, the cosmos is subdivided into heaven, earth, and hell. In shamanism, it is divided into upper, middle, and underworld. The Buddhist cosmology subdivides the individual levels in an even more differentiated way.

Except for the earth, all planes are subtle worlds. The earth is unique in its material form. According to Vedic cosmology, the earth is the last planet of the middle existence planes. From its current position, it is strongly influenced by dark and luminous forces at the same time.

The earth is considered to be a great transformation planet, on which all beings get the chance to go through great consciousness transformation processes within a short span of time.

This is special, because on other levels it takes much more time, to undergo this kind of transformation during one single lifespan. Every life on Earth is of great value and should be used with a great focus on the inner development. If we would constantly stay in this awareness, we would not waste time with insignificant things and would use the precious time that is given to us very well. Not every soul gets the permission to incarnate on earth and to go through this unique chance of developments.

In most spiritual traditions and religions, the luminous worlds are described as places of immeasurable joy, purity, freedom, and unconditional love. They are the home of all the luminous beings, like the arch-angels, the saints, the half-gods, and the gods.

Their consciousness is permeated by great love and selflessness. The hellish planes of existence are depicted as dark and fiery. There, dark beings are at home. These worlds are dominated by slavery and egoism.

In general, it can be said, that the higher the vibration frequency of the respective world, the more light, peace, nearness to God, joy, and holiness is in the consciousness of the living beings there. In relation to man that means that the more love, inner peace and selflessness he carries within himself, the higher his vibrational frequency and the more his consciousness resonates with the higher realms.

The lower the frequency vibration of the world, the more is the consciousness determined by egoism, violence, hatred, destruction, and negativity. The more selfishness and egoism a human being carries within himself, the lower his vibrational frequency is, and the more he is in resonance with the dark worlds. By inner work, man has the chance at any time to change the frequency of his consciousness and to follow the path of light.

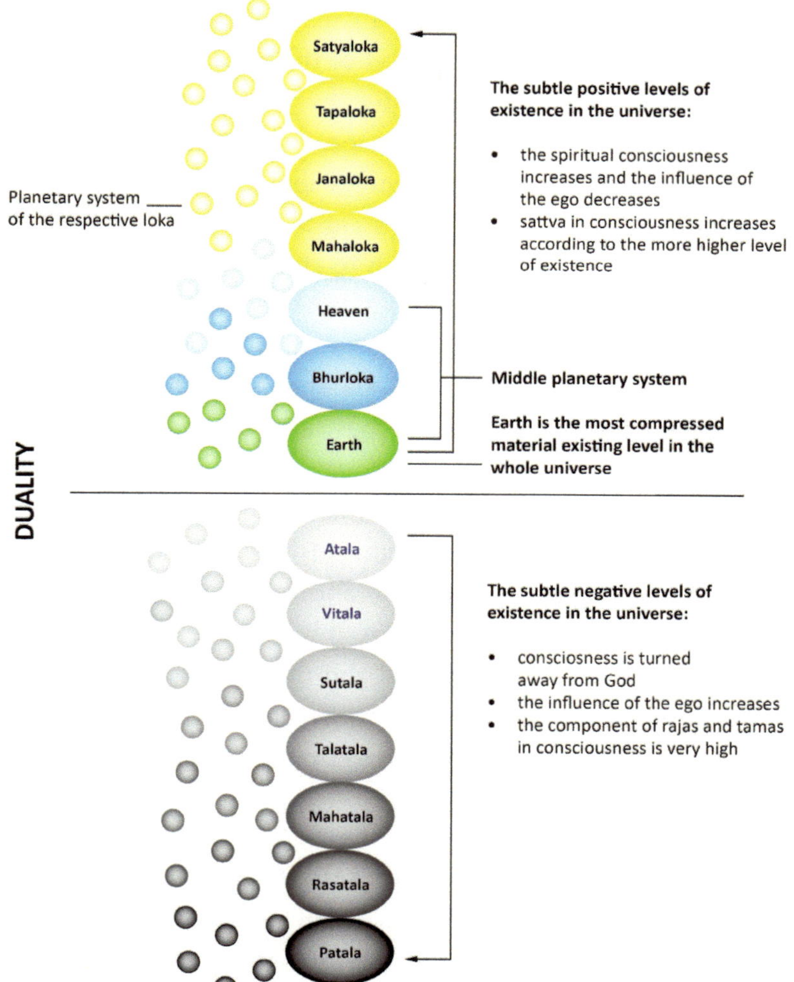

- According to the ancient Indian writings the universe exists of 14 different levels of existence.
- Each level of existence consists of own planets. They all exist here and now on a different perception frequency.

THE SEVEN POSITIVE AND NEGATIVE PLANES OF EXISTENCE IN NATURE

The divine consciousness is the cause of the existence of all existing planes. They are part of the creation game and they are permeated and united by the universal divine consciousness. The original divine source exists beyond these created worlds. To know about this cosmology reminds us of how very important it is to live an ethical life. It can exhort us and help us to give up selfishness and activities that nourish the dark side of life, like alcohol and drug consumption, watching horror movies, violence, and pornography. Instead of this, we should better dedicate ourselves to lightful activities that serve the well-being of all living beings.

Finally, the purpose of life is to seek God and to rediscover him within our hearts. Thereby we overcome the inner drought, depression, and emptiness that exist without his existence in our lives. It is the Spirit of God and his grace that revives the soul and fills it with light, love, harmony, peace, gentleness, joy, liveliness and creativity. To live in God means to rediscover one's own divinity and to be filled with the good.

COSMIC CYCLES – THE FOUR AGES

All happenings that occur on Earth are caused by two factors. On one hand, they are caused by the state of humanities consciousness and the kind of decisions they make. They decide between peace and war in the inside and the outside world. On the other hand, there are superordinate cosmic events like the cycles of nature which play an important role. For example the cycle of the seasons that can be experienced by every human being every year anew. The atmospheric conditions of the cycles are given by nature, for example, that leaves fall from the trees in autumn, or that it becomes cold in certain regions of the earth in wintertime. Mankind can only adapt to its circumstances.

In addition to the seasonal cycle, there exist much larger cycles in nature. Scientists know about that, but they are contradictory in their interpretations. The Vedic knowledge gives us a clear picture. Based on this background knowledge, the latest happenings in nature can be explained.

In the Vedas, the superordinate time cycles are called «Yugas». «Yuga» means «age» or «epoch». Altogether, there are four major time cycles, which the universe goes through. They are called «Satya Yuga» (Golden Age), «Treta Yuga» (Silver Age), «Dwarupa Yuga» (Bronze Age) and "Kali Yuga" (Age of Darkness). Like the seasons, they repeat themselves in ever-recurring order and are characterized by a certain mood in nature. A completed cycle is called «Maha Yuga», which means «great age».

The epochs differ in their duration. The Satya Yuga has duration of 1,782,000 million years. It is the longest period of time. The Kali Yuga last 432,000 years and is the shortest time period. There exist also other time specifications in literature. I would like to use as a model those which are already mentioned because they are in harmony with my experiences.

The ages also differ in their relationship between spiritual consciousness and ego-consciousness, in the collective consciousness of mankind on earth. In Satya Yuga, for example, nearly 100 percent of mankind lives in spiritual consciousness (soul consciousness). That means that humans live in harmony with God, the soul, and the natural laws. In Kali Yuga, the material age, the proportion is different. Here 75 percent of mankind lives in ego-consciousness and only 25 percent in soul consciousness.

Within a time period, it is possible that other ages can occur for a certain time. For example, the Kali Yuga lasts in total 432,000 years. Within this period of time a Satya Yuga, Treta Yuga, or Dwarupa Yuga can be possible, for of about 2,000-years duration each. However, the Kali Yuga remains the principle underlying movement. Within this time, the spiritual consciousness increases in the collective consciousness. But it will go down again when the period is over.

Further information about the various ages can be found in the following graphic. For us at this point, a closer consideration of the Kali Yuga and Satya Yuga is important.

KALIYUGA

More than 5000 years ago humanity entered into a Kali Yuga. From the perspective of consciousness, the darkest of all ages.

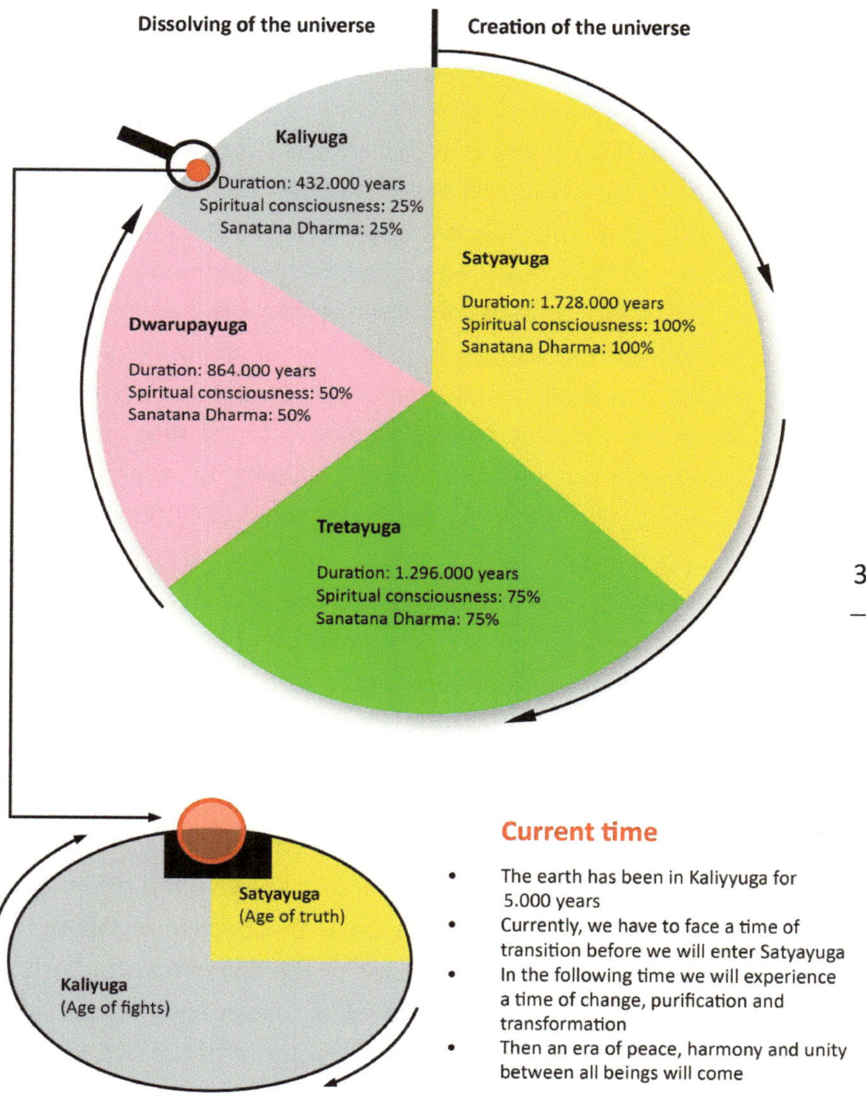

Current time

- The earth has been in Kaliyyuga for 5.000 years
- Currently, we have to face a time of transition before we will enter Satyayuga
- In the following time we will experience a time of change, purification and transformation
- Then an era of peace, harmony and unity between all beings will come

THE FOUR AGES OF THE UNIVERSE

The majority of humanity (75%) lives in ego-consciousness and only a small percentage of people are in spiritual consciousness (25%).

Most of the humans of this era are strongly attached to the material world and have forgotten their divine origin. They believe that the present life on earth is their only existence. They can't remember that being human is only an experience of their soul and not their real origin.

Their consciousness is in a kind of deep sleep. This means that their higher mental powers are not activated. There are scientific studies that have found that humans currently only use about 3-5 percent of their brain capacity. Who would we be if we would use 100 percent of our capacity?

Originally man and nature are ONE. In Satya Yuga, that unity is lived. In Kali Yuga the majority of people separate themselves from the divine source, because of egoism and ignorance. This is a reason why they also lose their access to their intuition. If a person loses the contact to the inner voice, he loses the contact to himself and can be influenced and conditioned from the outside.

Furthermore, this separation causes two different inner perspectives. On the one hand the perspective of the ego and on the other hand, the one of the divine nature. Both perspectives are potentially present in every human being.

The ego-directed man creates an artificial world in which he becomes the slave of his self-created ideas. This perspective doesn't have much in common with the divine reality. Because the ego-directed voice dominates in our current time, it is difficult for many people to leave it behind, because it is considered as normal.

Every healthy relationship consists of a balance between giving and taking. This is valid in interpersonal relationships as well as in our personal relationship with nature. In Kali Yuga, the relationship between man and nature falls completely out of balance. Man takes from earth without giving back to nature or being grateful for what he receives. Driven by profit, his perspective becomes short-term and short-sighted. Through the one-sided relationship and the ignorance of the laws of nature, which regulate the divine harmony and the order in the cosmos, he creates great imbalances in nature.

Within a very short time, man has now nearly destroyed the earth and himself. The whole mankind sits like a frog in the water, which slowly heats up. The bad thing is that many people are still looking away and are not willing to change their minds and actions. And even fewer people are ready to contribute, to really do something for a change of the situation in the world. They prefer to escape into the deceptive normality of everyday life and believe in the many lies they are surrounded by. Who would like to sincerely feel the pain when he awakens and realizes that as a part of the great whole, he is deeply disregarding and injuring himself, and other beings, with his behavior?

And so it goes on: Man kills billions of animals each year cruelly so that he can cover his unnecessary daily consumption of meat and fish. Ignorantly and blithely he looks over the unspeakable suffering that he does to his fellow creatures and also to the earth. A few days ago I heard in the news, that in 2015 in Germany alone, 45,000,000 million male chicks were shredded alive because they have no use for the poultry industry. Here, only madness can have entered.

Combined with the consumption of meat, man also exploits the arable land, because there is a great need for grains to feed the animals.

Man poisons his drinking water with antibiotics and hormones. He cuts down the rainforests which are the lungs of the earth. He has fished the seas almost empty and disposed of his garbage in the oceans. Man develops technologies that absorb his life energy. He is ruining himself by alcohol, drugs, cigarettes and an unhealthy lifestyle. He has developed an economy that is profitable and inhuman. In all corners of the earth violence and wars pop up. The list could be continued endlessly.

And all this is just happening to increase one's own well-being and comfort so that everything is available at any time and man has not to do without. Quantity, instead of quality! What price have we paid for it? And will have to pay in the future, if we do not reverse these developments?

In general, there is nothing wrong with creating things that make life better and easier. But if the production of technologies and food brings so much suffering to humans, animals and the earth, and the main motive behind it is only to increase the profit, and to run behind artificial papers and coins, then it is definitely a very big problem.

We live in an artificially created world that distracts us from the essence of life and does not allow us to connect with our true origin and vitality. We should be very aware of this.

A healthy economy means an economy for the well-being and happiness of all. This includes plants, animals, humans and the earth equally. This should be man's highest ideal.

According to the Law of Cause and Effect, which is also called the «Law of Karma» (Law of Energetic Balancing, to keep the harmony of the universe), everything we have done on this earth will return to us. Good and bad. Because of egoism, humanity has created a great negative collective karma, which has brought humanity very close to its own destruction. We have forgotten that the world was given to us to please us. We have never received the right to destroy planet Earth. If we destroy nature, we destroy ourselves. Nature has already begun to rebel.

Through our soul, the divine guides us and will let us know the solution for the way out of our misery. To be able to receive this knowledge, we have to devote ourselves to the inner path and to purify ourselves from egoism. The wonderful massage is that the Divine has never stopped to communicate with us. As soon as we turn the attention back inward and we give up our self-centeredness, we will be able to hear the inner voice again. If we follow that unconditionally, we return to the purity of our soul, and to inner fullness and joy, and we will receive guidance along our path.

INNER AND OUTER ENCOUNTER
FORCES AFFECT PEOPLE

First, we should become aware that man is a subtle energetic being that lives in a physical body. And that the material world, as it appears to us, is governed by subtle energetic principles. These subtle energies are perceptible to every human being in the form of thoughts and feelings. They exist, although they are not visible to most people and influence our well-being.

There exist forms of energy which are beneficial to us and increase our well-being, like love and gratitude. But there are also forms of energy that lower the energy field, like negative emotions such as anger, jealousy, and hatred.

Especially in Kali Yuga, man is confronted with many low-frequency energetic counterforces from within and outside. A great part is created by a human himself who did not act in harmony with nature. These include for example Karma and health problems.

This old stuff makes it difficult for him to connect continuously with the potential of his soul; it aggravates his own divinity. Because of their influence, therefore it is only possible to a limited extent for humans today to connect with their soul powers permanently. For that, first, he has to clear and liberate the path to his soul energetically.

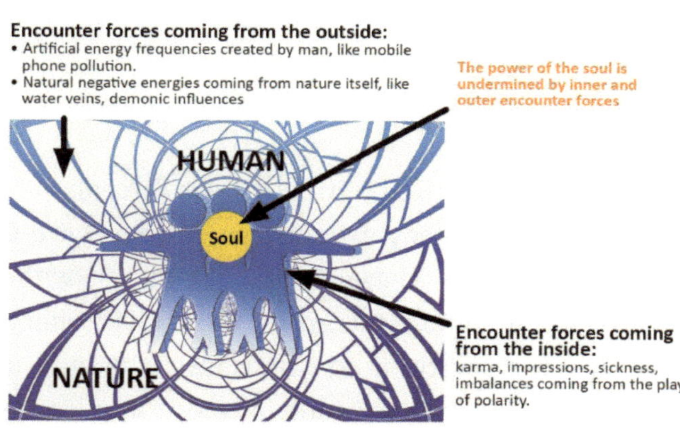

ENERGETIC SITUATION IN NATURE IN KALIYUGA

Internal counterforces are:

- Samskaras are stored in the subconscious mind. They are imprints and images caused by intensive and/or traumatic experiences. They result in destructive thought structures and emotions, such as anger, fear, shame, guilt, anger, jealousy and envy, which in turn lead to disharmonic reactions on situations.
- Disease
- Negative karma

External counterparts include:

- Environmental influences like contaminated water, contaminated food, air, and ground. They lower the human's frequency of consciousness.
- Artificially generated energy frequencies such as mobile and radio frequencies. They cover, like a veil, the collective field of consciousness of humans and prevent the connections to higher consciousness states.
- Natural negative forces coming from nature such as water veins.
- Influences by negative entities (Asurian forces).
- Everybody has already experienced the existence of one or more of these encounter-forces within himself and in different intensity. They cause energy loss, dim the clarity of consciousness and keep us captive in low-frequency consciousness, in a kind of a vibrational jail.

SATYA YUGA

«Satya» translated is «truthfulness». It is the «Golden Age» in which almost 100 percent of mankind lives in harmony with God, the soul and the laws of nature. The natural laws are called «Sanatana Dharma» in the Vedas. They are the everlasting and universal laws that regulate the coexistence in creation. The Sanatana Dharma is the foundation and essence of all religions and existed before any religious or spiritual traditions were established on earth.

In Satya Yuga, the natural laws are respected by all beings. Satya yuga is the age of the highest purity of mankind and the earth. Man is fully aware of his divine origin. Everything blossoms to its full beauty. Humans grow into their higher spiritual abilities and serve the creation.

The coexistence of people is characterized by cooperation and mutual support. Every living creature, including animals and plants, is considered an important part of a universal community. Interpersonal relationships and our relationship to nature are based on a healthy balance between giving and taking. Everything belongs to everyone and everyone thinks about the well-being of his fellow. Any form of relationship is free from attachment and carried by an inner attitude of freedom, unconditional love, understanding, well-being, unity, generosity, harmony, and peace. Encounters between people are brought together divinely. Communication and knowledge transfer can take place via telepathy and energy transmission.

All technologies that man develops in this age are in harmony with nature and the well-being of all living beings. According to this crystals play an important role. There exist an economic system that maintains the balance of the earth and the people.

Satya yuga is the era in which many spiritual masters return to earth.

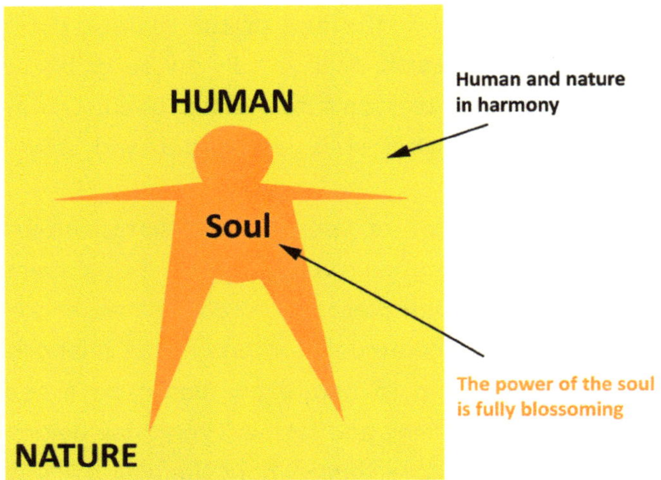

ENERGETICAL SITUATION OF NATURE AND MAN IN SATYAYUGA

TRANSITION FROM KALIYUGA TO SATYAYUGA

Everything in nature has a soul. Even planets are living beings that have a soul like humans. And as the soul of a man can energetically ascend or descend into a higher or lower vibrating form of existence, also planets can do so. Earth and mankind are currently in a phase of transition from a Kali Yuga, the energetically lowest frequency age, into a Satya Yuga, the energetically highest vibrating of all ages.

This Satya Yuga will be inserted for a temporally limited period of time, into the underlying Kali Yuga.

Dimensions of Consciousness

In our inner evolution process, we have to go through different stages of consciousness development. Each level of consciousness corresponds to a certain consciousness dimension. The higher the dimension the bigger are the possibilities and abilities of our consciousness. That means what is regarded as «normal» for the individual and the collective at one level of reality is now experiencing an expansion into a higher level of perception and reality, a new normal. The section of reality as it appears to us, got a larger frame, and also our understanding of greater contexts in nature have increased. In general, it can be said, the higher the vibrational frequency of the consciousness of a human being, the more spiritual he becomes and the more he comes in harmony with his original divine nature and understand the greater contexts of nature.

The dimensions of consciousness are not clearly distinguishable from one another and flow energetically into each other. That is the reason why in literature other data exists according to the number of dimensions. In the next consideration, I will start with the seven dimensions, because the current ascent process of the earth can be represented well with this model. This assumption is also commonly in general use.

In the first and second dimension of consciousness, man is instinctual and unconscious. His actions are based on his material and emotional need for satisfaction. At this point, man is not able to reflect on his thoughts and feelings.

In the third dimension of consciousness, a human starts to perceive himself in a social context and to act in it. His motives in social interaction are recognition and power. In the third dimension, man does not consciously perceive himself as the creator of his circumstances. The responsibility for inner emotional states is projected onto the outside world. Experiences are valued from the point of victim-perpetrator awareness. The awareness of this dimension is rigid, less flexible, and characterized by egotistical motives. Old injuries are held, and beliefs do not lose their validity until death. The period in which thoughts and desires become reality can last for many years.

From the fourth dimension of consciousness, man gradually begins to realize that through his way of thinking, speaking, and acting, he himself creates his reality and that his inner attitude determines what kind of experiences he draws into his life. The consciousness gets anchored in the presence and becomes lighter and more spontaneous. Man allows himself to change his opinions and attitudes according to his expanding knowledge. Unconditional love, as well as inner peace, becomes a continuous element of consciousness.

In the fifth dimension of consciousness, man becomes a conscious creator of his reality. His higher abilities are awakened, like the ability to telepathy. A person who has reached the fifth dimension of consciousness consciously chooses what he wants to manifest in reality. The basis of his action is unconditional love, understanding, compassion, freedom, harmony, and peace. Unloving behaviors can't exist at this level. The ability to control thoughts and feelings becomes very important at this level because there is no longer a time gap between thought and realization of the thought. Man is directly confronted with his own creations.

The sixth and seventh levels of consciousness are dimensions of enlightenment. Man is permanently anchored in the consciousness of God. He embodies love, goodness, wisdom, and harmony. Time and space begin to dissolve. He becomes a traveler and a servant of eternity.

According to this model, the collective consciousness of mankind was anchored until the beginning of the 1980s in the third dimension of consciousness. Up to this point, the individual could optionally decide whether to remain in the third dimension of consciousness or to rise to a higher level through inner work. Now the situation has changed. In the present time, the collective consciousness of mankind passes from the third into the fifth consciousness dimension. Through the decision of nature that the earth will rise into a higher form of consciousness, mankind is now called as a collective to go through an energetic purification and transformation.

A Misconception

The misperception and erroneous belief of many people is that they think they can continue as before. Unfortunately, this is a false thinking. Everyone is asked to do his inner work and to go through the lessons of the different dimensions of consciousness and to perfect them. On the way to the fifth dimension, we can´t take a shortcut and jump over the lessons of a dimension. The lessons of the fourth dimension must be learned and completed to be able to rise completely into the fifth dimension.

We can influence our development process by learning our lessons quickly and we can train ourselves in the qualities of the different dimensions at the same time.

Most people still have deep emotional and mental problems that come from the third dimension of consciousness and are stuck in it. The problem is that the «old ballast» weighs down the consciousness like a stone and prevents it from rising into higher dimensions.

Unfortunately, many people have not done their homework. One reason is the widespread ignorance and unbelief, which has become like a virus within the collective consciousness of mankind. This has caused that the processes in nature are already very advanced. Humanity is not in parallel and not where it could actually be standing.

PURIFICATION OF CONSCIOUSNESS

Consciousness can rise into a higher dimension when we purify ourselves from old mental structures and emotional injuries of the third consciousness dimension. Even, more so, when we develop the qualities of the soul and follow those impulses.

What during the purification process of consciousness happens can be precisely described with the «three gunas». All appearances of matter are penetrated by three subtle energies. They are called «tamas», «rajas» and «sattva». In any material and subtle form, they exist in different compositions. Tamas brings stability and solidity, rajas agility. Sattva is pure consciousness, information or light.

In the consciousness of man, sattva, rajas, and tamas produce different states of mind. They are dynamic and can dominate the inner experience. Rajas and tamas can cause imbalances when they dominate for a longer time.
Too much tamas can lead to depression, negativity, laziness and blocked spiritual energies. If rajas predominate nervousness, aggression, restlessness, impatience, and lack of concentration occurs. A person who has a lot of sattva in his consciousness has a balanced and harmonious state of mind. Sattva makes the mind peaceful, focused, joyful, harmonious, light, inspired and creative. In a sattvic state, man has access to his talents

and spiritual abilities and can unfold them. An example will show the three gunas more vividly:

If we give a human being a text to read, according to the prevailing guna in his mind, he will deal differently with the situation.

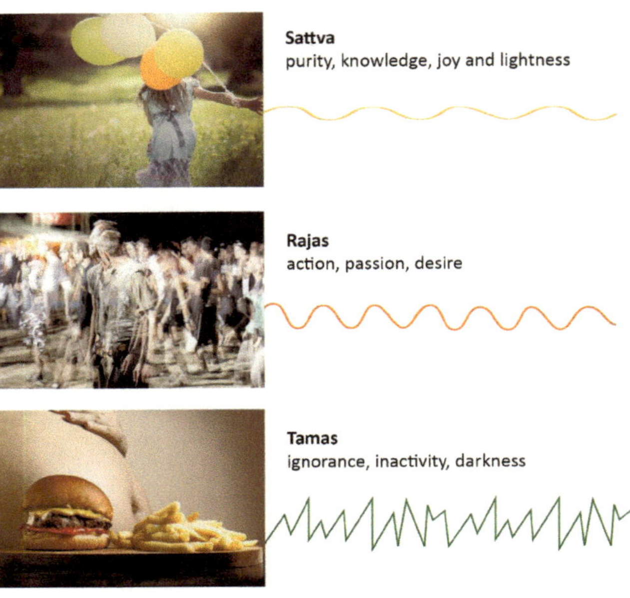

THE THREE GUNAS

If a person is in a state of mind of tamas, he is lazy and probably doesn´t want to read a book. In a state of mind of rajas, he suffers from a lack of concentration and will not be able to absorb or understand the information that he is reading in the book. Only in sattva, it is possible for him to read the book in a concentrated way and to record the read information.

If we talk about cleansing the consciousness, it is meant to remove tamas and rajas from consciousness, and to increase the proportion of sattva. This helps us to reach mental balance, to find inner peace, and to strengthen our intuitive ability.

INCREASE LIGHT IN CONSCIOUSNESS

Here are also a few pieces of food advice that support and speed up the purification processes:

- **Nourishment:** Our food has a very strong influence on our state of mind. It forms the kind of consciousness in a very determined way.

  Food, that increases sattva:
  - Fresh fruits and vegetables
  - Dry fruits
  - Nuts and seeds
  - Fresh milk products, like cream, ghee, curd, butter, buttermilk, milk (not pasteurized), sour milk, fresh cheese, etc.
  - Legumes
  - Grain
  - Honey
  - Not overeating
  - Keep the stomach one third should be left empty at mealtimes

Food that increases rajas:

- Coffee
- Black tea
- Cacao and chocolate
- Eggs
- Overmuch hot spices like chilli and pepper
- Too much salt
- Sugar
- White flour

Food that increases: tamas:

- Hard cheese
- Onion and garlic (but okay if used as medicine)
- mushrooms
- Meat and fish
- Drugs
- Alcohol
- Cigarettes
- Vinegar and Soya sauce
- Unripe, or overripe food
- Frozen food
- Canned food
- Food with preservatives and colourings
- Chemical medicine products (whoever has to take medicine because of his health state, should not take food that is tamasic.)
- Food that has been heated up many times.
- Overeating

Food from the tamas category should be completely avoided. Food that creates rajas should be reduced to a minimum. The main food that we take into ourselves should come from the sattva category.

- **Meditation**: During meditation, we can concentrate on the point between the eyebrows and chant a mantra like «OM» or «OM NAMAH SHIVAYA». It purifies the mind from negativity and disharmony.

- **Pranayama**: Breathing techniques from Yoga, like fire-breathing (Kapalabhati) and/or Anuloma Viloma.

- **Hatha-Yoga**: Hatha-Yoga harmonizes the dual energies in the body and leads to inner harmony, balance and mind control.

- **Maha Poorna Atma Yoga:** Maha Poorna Atma Yoga is a very simple technique to clear the consciousness from old mental and emotional patterns (Samskaras). Through the practice of Maha Poorna Atma Yoga, the light in consciousness strongly increases (sattva).

THE PURIFICATION PROCESS OF THE EARTH

As already mentioned, the earth and humanity will transit from a Kaliyuga into Satyayuga. From the darkest age to the highest. In this current transformation process, mankind has to generate maximum power from the energetic point of view. It has to dissolve all negativity and

53

egoism in its consciousness because Satya Yuga is the age of supreme purity of man and of the earth. We are called to free ourselves completely from the energetic imbalances of Kali Yugas. For this reason, we are currently in a kind of wash cycle, which allows us to accomplish these processes, but not only humans have to free themselves from the energetic imbalances of the Kali Yuga, but also so does the earth.

For this reason, there will be a cleansing process in the near future on earth in the form of a peak event. It marks the final change of the dimensions and cleans the earth from all negative energies and imbalances. This event enables the earth to enter into a new equilibrium state. The energetic equilibrium and the light quotient in the collective consciousness on earth in these days will determine how intensively this cleansing process will manifest on earth.

In various prophetic sources, this event is almost consistently described as a «three-day cleaning process» or «three-day darkness».

THE ESSENTIAL IN OVERVIEW

- The earth is close to transit from the third into the fifth dimension of consciousness. Earth and mankind will move from Kaliyuga into Satyayuga.
- The change of the dimensions will be connected with a three-day purification process of the earth. Through this,

humanity and nature will get the chance for a new beginning.

- It is of great importance for the ascension process to be inwardly prepared. We have to leave all our old ballast from the third dimension.
- The energetic balance of the earth and the level of light in the collective consciousness in those days will determine how intense the process of purification will have to be.
- After this change of the dimension, humanity will live in harmony with God, their own souls, and the laws of nature (Sanatana Dharma).
- Many spiritual masters will come back to earth.

Chapter 3
Prophecies
for the coming time

When I realized in September 2015 that the earth will really clean up and mankind and the earth will go through great upheavals in the coming time, it was at first a great challenge for me. Although I had felt it a long time before, a part of me resisted this imagination. It was just too gigantic. But the guidance of my spiritual teachers, Agastya Rishi and Lubamitra, made clear to me that it was true.

WE ARE THE CREATORS OF OUR FUTURE

As I mentioned earlier, after I had received the blessing for Two Minutes Yoga, in September 2015, I began to research because of my premonitions. To my astonishment, I found out that nearly all religious and spiritual traditions forecast a three-day purification process of the earth that would precede the turn of times.

First, it was not my intention to write down the different prophecies. But it became increasingly clear to me that their presentation fulfilled various important functions. On the one hand, it shows how universal the subject is, and it makes clear that it is cross-religious and unifying. On the other hand, the various prophecies contain important and useful suggestions about how we can prepare to be protected and to deal with the approaching challenges. Their portrayal also shows the urgency and relevance of the topic and makes clear how important a change in our way of thinking and acting is now. It also shows the background of the work of the 19 Siddhas, and of how important it is, in the current times.

I know that the confrontation with the prophecies first has something shocking and shaking up about it. But this aspect is an opportunity for everyone, if they do not choose fear as a reaction, to awaken from their paralysis, and then become active and creative, to start working for the improvement of the situation in the world. For now, there is still time to steer the ship in a different direction.

The future consists of probabilities that we shape through our state of consciousness and through our decisions. That is why the prophecies are changeable and have been partly changed. It is certain that the new age will come and that the earth will cleanse itself before. But how intense the purification process will manifest is decisively influenced by our current commitment or non-commitment. We sit as ONE humanity in a boat and are asked to work together to turn everything into good.

But if we continue to refuse and continue to hide behind a wall of ignorance, disbelief, and egoism, and if we do not wake up now, the transition into the new age will not be easy for us humans and will be associated with great challenges. The warning and call to change our behavior are mentioned in all prophecies. We are called to return to our own divinity and to the harmony within ourselves and nature.

Despite all the challenges that the transformation process involves, we should always keep in mind how it will benefit us. It will bring a healthy earth on which healthy people will live in harmony with nature. It is a revolution of love and peace. We have every reason for great anticipation!

Finally, I would like to point out that I can only take responsibility for the correctness of the information of my own process.

Perspective I:
Prophecies from Babaji

Interestingly, the book «Babaji Speaks Prophecies and Teaching» by Gertrud Reichel came to me in December 2015 at a time when I thought that this book here was already finished. Babaji's words gave me a deep access to my own experiences and insights.

After a phone call in December 2015, Gertraud Reichel allowed me to quote from her book and to share Babaji's powerful messages according to the end and the transition period, with the readers of this book.

April 16, 1977

«Babaji prophesied very bad times for mankind, and that from 1980 onwards the earth would suffer increasing destruction and disaster.» (p.19)

«Babaji advised everyone to stand with their religions and to follow the ancient teachings of the wise. In particular, he emphasized the singing of Om Namah Shivaya, as often as possible, regular discussions, singing and listening to religious songs, reading holy books, and explaining their importance to the benefit of the listeners.» (p.21)

«He instructed everyone to tell these words to others before it will be too late for mankind to ward off the coming disaster. Only those who take these principles seriously would survive.» (p.21)

July 26, 1979

«There will be a great change, through a bloody revolution. Peace will only come when the revolution has reached its peak. At the end of the destructive revolution, no country, whether big or small, will be spared. Some countries are completely extinguished; there remains no sign of their former existence. In other countries, 3-5 percent, a maximum of 25 percent of the population will survive.» (p.21)

«The destruction is caused by earthquakes, flooding, accidents, conflicts, and wars. Those who worship the God of their religion will be spared» (p.21)

July 28, 1979

«First, the destruction will take place, followed by a rest. After all, peace will prevail» (p.22)

«Prayer will be the only salvation, the only protection. Forget the past and the future, eradicate all other thoughts, and pray with a deep concentration of the mind and soul!» (p.22)

March 14, 1980

«When the new kingdom comes, many things will be much easier for you.» (p.24)

April 3, 1980

«Keep quiet during the catastrophe. Do not challenge me. Focus on the mantra: Om Namah Shivaya.» (p.24)

September 14, 1981

«Babaji was asked how other people could be helped during this time. He said, by announcing his appearance, by spreading his message. It is the first duty of every one to carry this message into the world.» (p.29)

December 16, 1981

«It is the duty of every one to be attentive and not to waste time unnecessarily. Do your duty! Do not be sluggish! This is the age of action.» (p.31)

«Forget your national origin. We are one here, a universal family. Have no feelings of a separate identity. Serve people with your mind, body, wealth, and understanding.» (p.31)

December 25, 1981

«Since the earth was created, God has always appeared to look at and protect the garden of this world. Thus he appears from time to time to weed the weeds, and direct the faithful and good men to the right path.» (p.33)

December 28, 1981

«Someone who does not work constructively is a dead man. Only those who work will survive the destruction. Do more than you need. A new kingdom will soon emerge, and only the one who is able to do karma-yoga will be able to survive. During the work, you should always repeat the mantra (prayer) of your choice. Nobody should lose courage, but always be brave» (p.37)

«Everyone who loves humanity is loved by others, is happy and will survive the destruction. Try to make this ideal clear to each individual.» (p.38)

«You should not hate anyone, disappoint anyone, help each other, and practice charity.» (P.38)

February 2, 1981

«You are the messenger of the revolution. Later you will be the messenger of peace, but first the revolution.» (p. 39)

March 25, 1982

«Mistakes of thousands of years are extinguished when we bow to God's feet when he touches us with a blessing.» (p.40)

«Now our hearts are prepared for the coming revolution so that we can contribute with serenity.» (p.40)

«Everyone has to regard himself as a humble servant of the world.» (p.44)

April 6, 1982

«In our free time, we should sing bhajans, religious songs, meditate, and repeat the name of God.» (p. 44)

May 5, 1982

«Here follows an overview of the future events: Punjab, West Bengal, and other Mohammedan countries will be completely destroyed. Some countries will disappear completely without a trace. The largest parts of America will be destroyed. Russia will survive by the grace of God, as it happened in ancient times» (p. 49)

«People will perish by toxic gases, but the buildings will stay.» (p.49)

August 17, 1982

«Every step you take will benefit the whole world.» (p.55)

«Don't fall back into your old habits, but progress. Karma Yoga is your highest duty.» (p.56)

December 24, 1982

«Wake up your fellow.» (p.63)

December 26, 1982

«You must all help to perfect mankind. By saving humanity, each individual will be saved.» (p.64)

«The time will come when you need to work to survive.» (p.65)

«What you feel now will become meaningless in the next moment. The time will come when cities emerge where the sea is now, and sea will be there where cities are now.» (p.65)

«This destruction will transform everything, nothing will remain as it was. You should leave your bond with this world. Only the repetition of the names of God will benefit you. Everything else is futile. God's names have more power than a thousand atomic and hydrogen bombs together.

Help yourself by repeating the name of God. You all know that the name of God is the highest. Why do you hang your thoughts on the transitory things of this world? Why don´t you spend your time in meditation and repeating the names of Gods? Bind to God!» (p.65-66)

January 5, 1983

«Don´t take drugs [...], with drugs there is no progress for you, but you remain stuck in your development. Learn to avoid drugs. Only then you can teach others» (p.67)

January 9, 1983

«Think and do good. Always have good thoughts!» (p.67)

«My plan is that salvation will only come to those who will do karma-yoga.» (p.68)

«How much money you may have, use it only for good purposes. Work, positive thinking and giving life to humanity is the best.» (p.68)

January 22, 1983

«No place shall remain without the prayer OM NAMAH SHIVAYA, Lord thy will be done. It must be known in every street, in every house.» (p.69)

«Everyone should follow the religion of their choice or go on his own way, the only important thing is to be human.» (p.70)

«Everyone has to look at his home country as a place of heaven and has to clear the idea of «I» and «mine» from his consciousness.» (p.70)

January 24, 1983

«The whole world will be ONE kingdom, there will be ONE king, and ONE law will rule over the whole world» (p.71)

January 29, 1983

«God can only live in cleanliness. Living in cleanliness is one of the most important steps to realize God.» (p.72)

«Everything must be clean, for cleanliness is the first step to reach God.» (p.73)

March 21, 1983

«A true man is the one who is doing his assigned work.»(p.74)

«Your character and attitude must be equally good. You must make your contribution to the great changes of this great revolution, no matter what country you come from.» (p.75)

March 22, 1983

«Awake! Rise! All of you must join and unite with people all over the world» (p.76)

April 7, 1983

«Be ready to help people wherever you are. Be strong as a rock, serious and deep as the sea. Think of the earth as a mother. The earth is one» (p.78)

«None of all that was invented will be useful. Everything can be destroyed» (p.78)

April 10, 1983

«On that day when all mankind becomes laborious, nothing will be missing in the world. Man must improve his situation through diligence.» (p.81)

May 24, 1983

«The only valid religion is humanity, which represents tolerance and forgiveness.» (p.9)

December 17, 1983

«Through this great upheaval, even the geography of the earth will change [...].» (p.152)

«Everything you do should be targeted. Use the time you would have wasted to travel here and there to do something good for a human being or any other living being.» (p.152)

«I don´t want you all to perish in this greatest revolution of the world history. The hearts of all those who hear or read of this revolution will melt. This is a time of tremendous destruction comparable to no other time.» (p.153)

«The countries that invented the destructive weapons will be destroyed. You must not believe you are safe. Secure is only who is with God.» (p.153)

«You must be able to work as fast as a machine, and your brain must think of mantras like a computer. Do not worry about things.» (p.154)

December 25, 1983

«Humanity today is in a very degenerate state: like marionettes, people dance for demonic puppeteers. We must protect people and give them wisdom and knowledge. We should not lose our courage.» (p.160)

February 4, 1984

«To turn your back to karma yoga and become lazy is the greatest danger you can go into.» (p.171)

January 31, 1984

«Everything can be realized on this earth if we are purposeful and diligent.» (p.168-169)

Perspective II:
European Prophecy

The Prophecy-Researcher Stephan Berndt

Stephan Berndt is a German future researcher. He collected in total 250 texts of European prophecy from the period 1100 to 1980. He extracted the individual prophecies and examined them according to overlaps. His scientific study was based on 5000 individual predictions. An analysis of the data reveals that the European prophecies essentially predict two major events: a third world war and «Three-day darkness». A possible third world war is not mentioned in all sources. However, the «three-day darkness» is predicted in all sources, except from one. A summary of the results of the study by Stephan Berndt can be found in the figure on p.69

Stephan Berndt has especially dealt with the German prophet and clairvoyant Alois Irlmaier, who had an outstanding visionary gift and had a high hit rate regarding the correctness of his predictions. In the following section, the person Alois Irlmaier and his prophecies will be presented.

Aussagen zu Teilaspekten der Dreitägigen Finsternis

#	Quellen mit Bezug zur Dreitägigen Finsternis	Zeit	Datensätze	Qualität	Finsternis			Krieg	Naturkatastrophen (Erklärung siehe nächste Seite)								Ratschläge			Literatur *
					3	F	W		~	P	E	N	Ü	O	D	V	H	F	T	
1	Irlmaier	1959	150	I																30/134
2	Biernacki	1984	149	IV																8/289
3	Seher v. Waldviertel	1959	79	II																12/262
4	Dixon	1970	48	IV																5/147
5	Kugelbeer	1922	43	III																15/101
6	Luecken	1972	38	III																8/231
7	Stockert	1948	37	III																12/221
8	Smith, T.H.	1991	34	III																71/68
9	Elena Aiello	1955	33	II																10/161
10	Zönnchen	1988	33	III																85/143
11	Lindenlied	1850	29	II																7/374
12	Uriella	1993	21	IV																209/17
13	De la Vega	1982	18	III																16/214
14	M. J. Jahenny	1938	16	III																8/208
15	Böhmischer Seher	1940	16	III																8/46
16	Pater Pio	1961	14	I																8/151
17	Taigi	1837	12	II																8/132
18	Quelle aus Hadith	~800	10	II																99/94
19	Heilige Ottilie	720	7	II																14/75
20	Ashtar Sheran	1997	7	III																PaB
21	Palma v. Oria	1872	6	III																24/53
22	M. Bergadieu	1875	6	III																88/315
23	Johannes Friede	1948	6	II																46/84
24	Baourdi	1878	6	III																10/154
25	Schweizer Neuoffenb.	1856	4	III																14/107
26	Henle	1890	4	III																8/275
27	J. d. la Faudaise	1819	2	III																4/170
28	Gründ.d Kongr.v k.Bl	1837	2	III																10/155
29	Heroldsbach (Heilm.)	1949	1	III																8/275
30	Nostradamus	1558	548	II																1/377
31	Korkowski	1947	178	III																32/23
32	La Salette	1846	84	II																7/367
33	Erna Stieglitz	1972	50	III																12/237
34	Lorber	1864	33	II																5/156
35	Madam Sylvia	1934	24	III																14/178
36	Birger Claesson	1950	23	II																PaB
37	Frau aus Valdes	1968	20	II																PaB
38	Methodius v. Patara	677	20	III																5/139
39	C. v. Heisterbach	1230	20	II																15b/63
40	Italienische Sibylle	100	19	III																5/209
41	Hep. v. St. Gallen	1081	18	I																41/85
42	Marienth. Klosterbuch	1749	18	III																41/245
43	Libysche Sibylle	-200	16	III																5/205
44	Edda	1300	14	III																14/59
45	Emmerick	1822	13	III																14/77
46	Amsterd. Botschaft	1947	12	III																PaB
47	Beliante	1923	11	III																14/73
48	Mutter Graf	1961	10	III																60/123
49	Handwercher	1830	8	III																8/191
50	Maya-Quelle	1500	8	III																77/118
51	Hopi-Quelle	1938	7	II																S.99
52	Bertha Dudde	1947	7	III																19/55
53	Kossuthány	1918	6	III																47/407
54	Higginson	1880	4	III																24/81
55	Kerizinen	1965	3	III																8/252
56	Mongolische Quelle	1700	2	III																99/98

* teilweise zu einzelnen Quellen weitere Literaturangaben nötig – Literaturcodes siehe Seite 368

Prediction of the three-day purification process. On the left side, you see the name of the prophet. In the third column at which time it was predicted. The fourth column shows how many prediction data exist from that person. In the fifth column, Stephan Berndt values the quality of the prediction. Category one is the most reliable. In the next column, you can see if the respective prophet predicted the three-day purification process or not. There is a column in which the prophets who have predicted it is marked in black. The ninth column shows the prediction of a third World War.

ALOIS IRLMAIER

Alois Irlmaier was in his lifetime, a well-known well builder, who lived near Munich. He was born in 1894 and died in 1959 in Freilassing. Through his profound abilities, he was able to find water sources via body sensations. He was also clairvoyant.

At the end of World War II, Alois Irlmaier was able to help many people by telling them if their family members would return alive from war, or if they have already died. Alois Irlmaier's prophecies are mainly about possible events in Germany. The following details are based on the book by Stephan Berndt: «Alois Irlmaier - A man says what he sees».

Alois Irlmaier predicts two great events for the earth and mankind, on one hand, a third-world war and on the other hand, three-day darkness. Both events should follow on, from one another immediately. The year of this happening is preceded by a particularly mild winter and a profitable harvest. Alois Irlmaier describes a possible beginning of a third world war in July / August of the respective year.

On a cold winter night of the same year in the months of November or December suddenly a loud thunder would be heard. This would be the sign that the three-day darkness begins. When the thunder is heard, one should remain in the house and immediately close all windows and doors and make them both light and airtight. The whole of the windows can be compacted with the paper of newspapers, and the windows can be covered with black foil. One should also avoid looking out of the window out of curiosity. This could be deadly. For the coming days, one should not leave the house and pray deeply. All people who live in a holy place will be protected. Heaven will care for them.

Presages of the three-day darkness, that Alois Irlmaier mentions:

1. «First comes prosperity as never before.
2. This is followed by a loss of faith as has never happened before.
3. Thereupon, there will be an unprecedented loss of morality that has never existed before.
4. Then a great number of strangers will enter the country.
5. There is high inflation.
6. Soon afterward revolution follows. [Germany, Italy, France] [...]» (Berndt, p.87)

Recommendations for the three-day darkness from Alois Irlmaier:

- One should pray deeply. Even people who have no relationship with God should simply turn to God and pray for the good of all beings and as little suffering as possible!
- You should light consecrated candles.

- Windows should be darkened with black view protection.
- The windows and doors should be airtightly sealed with newspaper.
- Supplies should be there for at least three months. The food should not be stored in glasses, but only in sealed stainless steel cans.
- Outside the house, you should not eat or drink. The Divine will take care of the well-being of all who are in confidence.
- You should store as much water as possible. Tap water can be used.
- After the three-day darkness, you should not leave the house for about three weeks because of the danger of looting.
- One should keep away from big cities. There it will be worst.
- Marine regions should be avoided.

According to Alois Irlmaier, after the three-day darkness, the climate in Germany will drastically change. There will be temperatures as they are currently in southern Italy. In Germany, oranges would grow and there would be no winter.

About one year after these happenings it would be very challenging for people. Then a time of long peace will come and people will be happy. Everyone has as much land as he can cultivate with his own hands.

Technologically humanity would fall back into the nineteenth century.

At this point, I would like to supplement Babaji's view of possible events in Germany. According to the book «Blessing of Babaji» from the author, Renata Caddy, Germany will not experience a war but will be affected by natural disasters.

Perspective III: American Prophecy

Also in American prophecy, there are various sources that predict the 3-day purification process.

Edgar Cayce

Edgar Cayce was a world known seer who entered the world's history as the «sleeping prophet». He lived from 1877 to 1945. Edgar Cayce counseled many people during his lifetime. He also predicted coming happenings in the close future on earth and for humanity. Before he started a sitting he went into trance. Then, he received information from the universal knowledge field and the Akashic Record. He himself could not remember during and after the sessions, what had happened in the time of his trance and what kind of information he had received. Later the sittings were written down by his wife.

There probably is no other prophet in the world who has left such an amount of documented settings as Edgar Cayce. In the library of Edgar Cayce's «Association for Research and Enlightenment» organization in the USA, about 14,300 documents are being kept.

In his sessions, Edgar Cayce spoke about all kinds of issues concerning the physical and subtle world. He also gave medical advice, which must have even impressed doctors, because Edgar Cayce had no medical training. In these meetings, he spoke like a doctor and gave advice according to operations, naturopathy, and so on. Cayce is esteemed also as a great healer. There are numerous third-party publications about him.

Edgar Cayce also saw gigantic events coming to the earth. He forecast catastrophes, which would go far beyond man's imagination. He described, amongst other things, that Japan and large parts of the South-East of America would disappear into the sea and that Europe would change within a short time its geography and climate. This would be the result of a pole shift.

DRUNVALO MELCHIZEDEK

Drunvalo Melchizedek is an internationally known spiritual teacher who lives with his wife in Sedona, USA. He studied mathematics and physics at the Berkeley University of Arts. He finished his studies one semester before graduation to devote his life entirely to the spiritual path. He has written about the experiences of his journey in the famous books «The Flower of Life, in two volumes» and the «Snake of Light».

According to own statements, Drunvalo Melchizedek was able to learn from many spiritual traditions and native people worldwide. By connecting the collected knowledge, he has created a universal path of awakening and founded the «School of Remembering». He also predicts a pole shift and gigantic changes that will be connected with this happening. He especially refers to the prophecies of the Maya and of other native people. According to Drunvalo Melchizedek, the prophecies are one in their essence.

PERSPECTIVE IV: CHRISTIAN PROPHECIES

In the Bible, the end time of the current age is already announced more than 2,000 years ago. It contains a series of warnings and signs that indicate great upheavals on earth and predictions about the return of Jesus. The Bible quotations were taken from the online Bible Gateway from King James version: https://www.biblegateway.com/

BIBEL VERSES

Isaiah Chapter 24, 1-6, 15-20
The coming judgement of God on earth

[1] Behold, the LORD maketh the earth empty, and maketh it waste, and turneth it upside down, and scattereth abroad the inhabitants thereof. [2] And it shall be, as with the people, so with the priest; as with the servant, so with his master; as with the maid, so with her mistress; as with the buyer, so with the seller; as with the lender, so with the borrower; as with the taker of usury, so with the giver of usury to him. [3] The land shall be utterly emptied, and utterly spoiled: for the LORD hath spoken this word. [4] The earth mourneth and fadeth away, the world languisheth and fadeth away, the haughty people of the earth do languish. [5] The earth also is defiled under the inhabitants thereof; because they have transgressed the laws, changed the ordinance, broken the everlasting

covenant. [6] Therefore hath the curse devoured the earth, and they that dwell therein are desolate: therefore the inhabitants of the earth are burned, and few men left.Wherefore glorify ye the LORD in the fires, even the name of the LORD God of Israel in the isles of the sea. [16] From the uttermost part of the earth have we heard songs, even glory to the righteous. But I said, My leanness, my leanness, woe unto me! the treacherous dealers have dealt treacherously; yea, the treacherous dealers have dealt very treacherously. [17] Fear, and the pit, and the snare are upon thee, O inhabitant of the earth. [18] And it shall come to pass, that he who fleeth from the noise of the fear shall fall into the pit; and he that cometh up out of the midst of the pit shall be taken in the snare: for the windows from on high are open, and the foundations of the earth do shake. [19] The earth is utterly broken down, the earth is clean dissolved, the earth is moved exceedingly. [20] The earth shall reel to and fro like a drunkard, and shall be removed like a cottage, and the transgression thereof shall be heavy upon it, and it shall fall, and not rise again.

Matthew Chapter 24, 1-51

[1] And Jesus went out, and departed from the temple: and his disciples came to him for to shew him the buildings of the temple. [2] And Jesus said unto them, See ye not all these things? verily I say unto you, There shall not be left here

one stone upon another, that shall not be thrown down. [3] And as he sat upon the mount of Olives, the disciples came unto him privately, saying, Tell us, when shall these things be? and what shall be the sign of thy coming, and of the end of the world? [4] And Jesus answered and said unto them, Take heed that no man deceive you. [5] For many shall come in my name, saying, I am Christ; and shall deceive many. [6] And ye shall hear of wars and rumours of wars: see that ye be not troubled: for all these things must come to pass, but the end is not yet. [7] For nation shall rise against nation, and kingdom against kingdom: and there shall be famines, and pestilences, and earthquakes, in divers places. [8] All these are the beginning of sorrows. [9] Then shall they deliver you up to be afflicted, and shall kill you: and ye shall be hated of all nations for my name's sake. [10] And then shall many be offended, and shall betray one another, and shall hate one another. [11] And many false prophets shall rise, and shall deceive many. [12] And because iniquity shall abound, the love of many shall wax cold. [13] But he that shall endure unto the end, the same shall be saved. [14] And this gospel of the kingdom shall be preached in all the world for a witness unto all nations; and then shall the end come. [15] When ye, therefore, shall see the abomination of desolation, spoken of by Daniel the prophet, stand in the holy place, (whoso readeth, let him understand:) [16] Then let them which be in Judaea flee into the mountains: [17] Let him which is on the housetop not come down to take anything out of his house:[18] Neither let him which is in the field return back to take his clothes.[19] And woe unto them that are with child, and to them that give suck in those days![20] But pray ye that your flight be not in the winter, neither on the sabbath day:[21] For then shall be great tribulation, such as was not since the beginning of the world to this time, no, nor ever shall be.[22] And except those days should be shortened, there should no flesh be saved: but for the elect's sake those days shall be shortened.[23] Then if any man shall say unto you, Lo, here is Christ, or there; believe it not.[24] For there shall arise false Christs, and false prophets, and shall shew great signs and wonders; insomuch that, if it were possible, they shall deceive the very elect.[25] Behold, I have told you before.[26] Wherefore if they shall say unto you, Behold, he is in the desert; go not forth: behold, he is in the secret chambers; believe it not.[27] For as the lightning cometh out of the east, and shineth even unto the west, so shall also the coming of the Son of man be.[28] For wheresoever the carcass is, there will the eagles be gathered together.

The coming of the son of man

[29] Immediately after the tribulation of those days shall the sun be darkened, and the moon shall not give her light, and the stars shall fall from heaven, and the powers of the heavens shall be shaken:[30] And then shall appear the sign of the Son of man in heaven: and then shall all the tribes

of the earth mourn, and they shall see the Son of man coming in the clouds of heaven with power and great glory.[31] And he shall send his angels with a great sound of a trumpet, and they shall gather together his elect from the four winds, from one end of heaven to the other.

Warning for Vigilance

[32] Now learn a parable of the fig tree; When his branch is yet tender, and putteth forth leaves, ye know that summer is nigh:[33] So likewise ye, when ye shall see all these things, know that it is near, even at the doors.[34] Verily I say unto you, This generation shall not pass, till all these things be fulfilled.[35] Heaven and earth shall pass away, but my words shall not pass away.[36] But of that day and hour knoweth no man, no, not the angels of heaven, but my Father only.[37] But as the days of Noah were, so shall also the coming of the Son of man be.[38] For as in the days that were before the flood they were eating and drinking, marrying and giving in marriage, until the day that Noe entered into the ark,[39] And knew not until the flood came, and took them all away; so shall also the coming of the Son of man be.[40] Then shall two be in the field; the one shall be taken, and the other left.[41] Two women shall be grinding at the mill; the one shall be taken, and the other left.[42] Watch therefore: for ye know not what hour your Lord doth come.[43] But know this, that if the goodman of the house had known in what watch the

thief would come, he would have watched, and would not have suffered his house to be broken up.

About the faithful and the evil servant

[44] Therefore be ye also ready: for in such an hour as ye think not the Son of man cometh. [45] Who then is a faithful and wise servant, whom his lord hath made ruler over his household, to give them meat in due season? [46] Blessed is that servant, whom his lord when he cometh shall find so doing. [47] Verily I say unto you, That he shall make him ruler over all his goods. [48] But and if that evil servant shall say in his heart, My lord delayeth his coming; [49] And shall begin to smite his fellow-servants, and to eat and drink with the drunken; [50] The lord of that servant shall come in a day when he looketh not for him, and in an hour that he is not aware of, [51] And shall cut him asunder, and appoint him his portion with the hypocrites: there shall be weeping and gnashing of teeth.

Lukas 21, 25-35

The coming of the Son of Man

[25] And there shall be signs in the sun, and in the moon, and in the stars; and upon the earth distress of nations, with perplexity; the sea and the waves roaring. [26] Men's hearts failing them for fear, and for looking after those things which are coming on the earth: for the powers of heaven

shall be shaken. [27] And then shall they see the Son of man coming in a cloud with power and great glory. [28] And when these things begin to come to pass, then look up, and lift up your heads; for your redemption draweth nigh.

From the fig tree

[29] And he spake to them a parable; Behold the fig tree, and all the trees; [30] When they now shoot forth, ye see and know of your own selves that summer is now nigh at hand. [31] So likewise ye, when ye see these things come to pass, know ye that the kingdom of God is nigh at hand.

Warning for Vigilance

[32] Verily I say unto you, This generation shall not pass away, till all be fulfilled. [33] Heaven and earth shall pass away: but my words shall not pass away. [34] And take heed to yourselves, lest at any time your hearts be overcharged with surfeiting, and drunkenness, and cares of this life, and so that day come upon you unawares. [35] For as a snare shall it come on all them that dwell on the face of the whole earth. [36] Watch ye therefore, and pray always, that ye may be accounted worthy to escape all these things that shall come to pass, and to stand before the Son of man.

2 Timotheus 3, 1-9
The decay of piety in the end time

[1] This is known also, that in the last days perilous times shall come. [2] For men shall be lovers of their own selves, covetous, boasters, proud, blasphemers, disobedient to parents, unthankful, unholy, [3] Without natural affection, trucebreakers, false accusers, incontinent, fierce, despisers of those that are good, [4] Traitors, heady, highminded, lovers of pleasures more than lovers of God; [5] Having a form of godliness, but denying the power thereof: from such turn away. [6] For of this sort are they which creep into houses, and lead captive silly women laden with sins, led away with divers lusts, [7] Ever learning, and never able to come to the knowledge of the truth. [8] Now as Jannes and Jambres withstood Moses, so do these also resist the truth: men of corrupt minds, reprobate concerning the faith. [9] But they shall proceed no further: for their folly shall be manifest unto all men, as their's also was.

Further Christian Sources

Vassula Ryden

In my research, I found the Christian mystic Vassula Ryden. Vassula Ryden was born in Greek. Her original family belongs to the Greek Orthodox Church. She was already clairvoyant as a child. She is married to a Swedish Protestant. They have two sons. Because of her husband´s profession, she and her family lived in different countries, including South Africa and Bangladesh.

Vassula Ryden lived a «normal life» up to the day when she wrote, as usual, a shopping list. Suddenly a supernatural force took over the writing of her hand and wrote a message on the paper in front of her. The supernatural power presented itself as her protective angel. The guardian angel had the task to prepare Vassula Ryden for the direct guidance of Jesus, God, the Holy Spirit and the Divine Mother Mary.

Jesus instructed her to work on the union of the fragmented churches because it would be the wish of God that all churches become One and ecumenical. For about 23 years she receives messages and gives lectures around the world. She is the founder of the movement «True Life in God».

Several years ago Vassula Ryden received the message that a new world is going to come. The transition into the new world would involve a great destruction if we wouldn´t change our egotistical behavior. On youtube, there exists a multi-part video series called «True Life in God». It starts with 1A. In the videos, she talks about how we are able to live with God in an intimate relationship. In one of these episodes, she reports, among other things, that Jesus had told her that the great upheavals on earth would come «soon». Vassula Ryden then asked Jesus: «Do you mean my ´soon or your ´soon´?» Because «soon» means something else from the perspective of eternity than from the perspective of humanity. Then Jesus answered her, «Your soon.»

It is interesting to mention that Vassula Ryden gives attention to Russia for a whole series. Jesus shared with her, that he would hold his protecting and blessing hands above Russia. Russia would play a main role in spirituality in the future world.

THE PASTOR ANDREAS BERGESLOW

Andreas Bergeslow is a Siberian pastor who lives in Germany. One day on a mission in Siberia, he had a heavy car accident and died. After five hours of death, he returned to his body. Because of his inner injuries, it is a miracle that he is still alive. During his death, he had a near-death experience. He left his body and met Jesus. Jesus instructed him to wake up the people and to show them the way to the light. Many people would currently choose their way into the dark worlds because of their egoism.

THE PASTOR RICK RENNER

Pastor Rick Renner reports in March 2015 about different visions he had in Sid Roth's TV- Series «It's Supernatural». In one vision he was called to Russia, where he is currently living with his family. In another one, an angel appeared to him and showed him how the earth will shake.

THE CHRISTIAN MYSTIC
ANGELICA ZAMBRANO

The at that time 16-year-old Christian mystic Angelica Zambrano from Ecuador fasted and prayed with her parents for ten days, as part of a Christian retreat. In November of that year, and after numerous preparations, she was guided by God through a dying process. She left her body for 23 hours. At this time God showed her the heavenly and hellish worlds. Before returning, she was commissioned by God to share her experiences with the world. She should warn the people and ask them to walk in the path of light.

PERSPECTIVE V:
FROM THE VIEW OF THE HOPIS

On his homepage (see bibliography), Gerd Gutemann summarizes the prophecies of the Hopi Indians from different sources. If you like to go more deeply into it, you can follow the recommendations of literature on his homepage. In the following, I would like to present the prophecies of the Hopi-Elder Dan Katchongva. They were published in 1970, two years before he died.

Dan Katchongva predicted two major events to mankind. On one hand, he foresaw a third world war and the destruction of great parts of the USA. On the other hand, days of purification, in which humanity and the earth would be purified by God. Those who survive this time would experience a new, wonderful world. There will be brotherhood and peace between men. All races were one family and would speak one language.

Happenings of the purification

«Our teachings and prophecies say that we must pay attention to the signs and omens that come and that will strengthen our faith. [...] Nature will speak with the enormous breath of the wind. There will be major catastrophes caused by earthquakes and floods. The weather and the seasons will change. Wild animals and plants will disappear and famine occurs. Like powerful storms, wars will arise. From the very beginning of creation, all of that was planned»

Third World War by «Red» [Communists] as the Cleanser

«The third event depends on the red symbol, which will take the command and will start to bring the four forces of nature in motion. When these forces are in motion, the whole world will be shaken [...]. The day of cleansing will come to all men. This war becomes ruthless [...]. We can´t be outside. We must stay in our houses. It will gather the evil people.»

«The cleaner will recognize everyone by his way of life, his head or the shape of his village and his house [...]. This cleansing will be for all honest people, the earth, and all living creatures. The sick on earth will be healed.»

Peace and harmony after the purification

«Mother Earth will blossom again and all people will be united in peace and harmony for a long time.»

«This is the universal plan, spoken by the great spirit at the beginning of time.»

Task of the Hopi

«The Hopi settled down on this part of the earth to care about this country with their ceremonial duties like other people settle elsewhere on the earth to care about the earth in their own way. Together they keep the world in balance.»

Decisive people of the purification

«We know of people who are intended to move the purification forward. It is the universal plan from the beginning of creation. Everywhere in the world, on different continents, it can be found drawn on rocks. If people around the world know about it, we will come together. Therefore, we ask you to spread these words everywhere so that people know about them.»

Wish of spreading these prophecies

«I have spoken. I wish this message to spread to all corners of this land and even over the great waters, where understanding people reflect the words of wisdom. This is my will. People can have different opinions on different things. But according to the nature of faith, on which the Hopi life is based, I expect, that at least one, if not two, agrees. If there are three, it means a lot.»

PERSPECTIVE VI:
THE VIEW OF A JEWISH BOY

In 2015, a Jewish boy named Nathan had a near-death experience on the Day of the Blood Moon. During his death, the potential future events on earth were shown to him in the spiritual world. He also foresaw a third world war and major changes in the world through natural catastrophes. He could decide if he wanted to stay on the other side or return to earth. He decided to come back to warn the people. Before his experience, he had nothing to do with religion. Only after this happening, he attracted the attention of the rabbis and the media.

PERSPECTIVE VII:
FROM THE VIEW OF NOSTRADAMUS

Rose Stern is a book author who has devoted her work in the past two decades to the decoding of the 1000 verses of the prophetic script of Nostradamus. A few years ago, she found another important key that gave her deeper access to this text. She found out that Nostradamus predicted a pole shift and according to this a great catastrophe that would come over the world. Nostradamus also mentions a third world war that could precede this event.

According to the data from the NCEI National Center for Environmental Information, which I am allowed to use with the kind permission of the NCEI in this context, the pole has almost doubled its speed over the last 20 years compared to the previous 90 years (see Figures on p.95). Some scientists assume that the pole will arrive in Siberia in the next 50 years and will stop there without major turbulences for man and earth. The perspective of Nostradamus is different. He describes that first, the pole will slowly move forward. Then suddenly it will make a right-angled jump of about 2000 km towards the Bering Strait. The leap would be the cause that the earth would start to shake.

By decoding the text of Nostradamus, Rose Stern was able to decipher the following text passage: «The great engine moves the centuries, sea, earth, people, their condition will change. The century of renewal will approach. The North Pole will change. [...] The great lightning will fall down on daytime. A large fire will fall from the sky in three nights. A little later the earth will tremble [...]» (Stern, pp.128-131).

In his verses, Nostradamus describes in details what might happen during the pole shift. If you want to know more about this, you can read the book of Rosen Stern «Nostradamus, The Divine Prophecy. Now!» (available only in German)

According to these happenings, Nostradamus also mentions a purification process for mankind. «The catastrophe, the astounding collapse of the magnetosphere will wash the earth» (Stern, p.185) and further «The past will be extinguished» (Stern, p.186). According to Rose Stern, the pole shift would be the answer of the Divine to the current situation. It will bring the decisive salvation on earth and enable mankind to live a healthy future. Humanity would no longer be able to reverse its own mistakes in nature by their own effort.

Nostradamus sees the inner and spiritual preparation of great necessity. It would be important to calm down the mind, to control the thoughts and to keep calm.

Perspective VIII:
From a Scientific View

It is known to science that pole shifts happen at certain intervals of time. But yet it does not have the technical possibilities to define precisely these intervals. Native people, like the Mayans, describe that pole shifts occur every 24,000 years. Scientists assume that the periods are longer, but they had to revise their data a few times in the past. This becomes clear in two different online newspaper articles in the German magazine «The World» from the years 1995 and 2010. According to this, in 1995 the scientists claimed that a pole shift would take every 800,000 years place. The next one would be expected in about 2,000 years. 15 years later, the data are revised in another article. In this, the scientists assume that a pole shift will be every 250,000 years. The next is overdue.

Through measurements, scientists could found out that the magnetic field of the earth has become weaker and weaker, for quite some time now. Several decades ago, the poles have already left their places of origin (see data from NCEI). Its movement has increased its speed in the last years. Currently, it is moving towards Siberia. Its arrival is expected in about 50 years.

If you would like to know more about the pole shift from a scientific perspective, you can watch the following film recommendation on YouTube: «Magnetic change: the poles are crazy» (available only in German). In this movie, the pole shift is explained in an interesting and simple way. From a scientific point of view, the state of the earth is also affected by the current state of the pole´s movement.

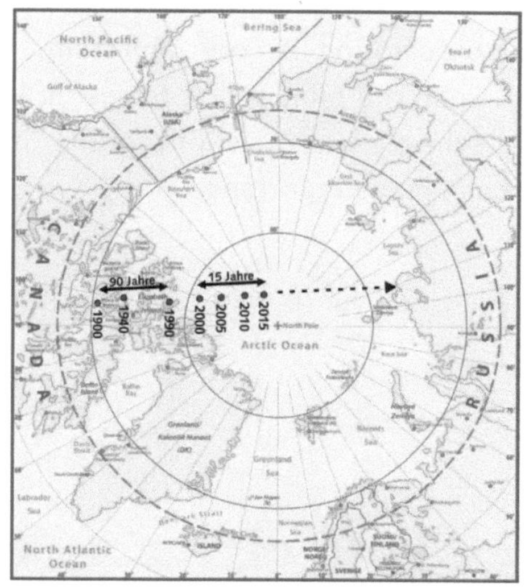

ACCELERATION OF THE POLE MIGRATION IN THE LAST 90 AND 15 YEARS

Summary of the Essential

- Many prophetic sources talk about a third World War that could precede the purification process.
- The three-day cleaning process could be caused by a pole shift which could lead to geographical and climatic changes.
- The internal preparation is very important. We should learn how to keep the mind quiet, to rest in inner peace and to liberate the consciousness of egoism.
- Prayers will be of great importance.

Chapter 4
Healing for the earth
The work of the 19 Siddhas

Siddha means «perfection». A Siddha is a being that has realized the supreme divine consciousness and works out of the highest frequencies of creation. Since ancient times, they have been universal teachers working from the highest levels of consciousness for the protection of the energetic equilibrium of humans and the earth. A Siddha lives in perfect harmony with the creation. He is God-like regarding his powers and can influence the natural laws for the benefit of all. Their work and their essence are permeated by the highest light, by purest intentions and unconditional love.

THE 19 SIDDHAS ARE PART OF UNITY

It is important to understand that from the point of the divine perspective only ONE nature and ONE humanity exist. Depending on the spiritual or religious tradition, this ONE reality is more or less described in different terminology. Therefore, a distinction between the different religious and spiritual traditions and fighting for right and wrong is a complete nonsense.

The 19 Siddhas are also part of the cosmic unity and they fulfill, like other spiritual masters and beings, individual and unique tasks in the universal transformation and ascension process of the earth. Their work is an important part of a great teamwork. At the present time, their work is of particular importance.

A GREAT CHANCE FOR HUMANITY

As already mentioned, the nature and man are closely connected through an all-embracing energy field of consciousness. All actions we do as individuals, which include thinking, speaking and acting, have an energetic influence on the collective field of consciousness. Through this field of consciousness, we create the happenings on earth, through the state of our energy. If we are in balance, if we live harmoniously with nature and it´s laws, and if we have developed spiritual qualities like love, compassion, understanding, and forgiveness, we create a positive energy field and strengthen the equilibrium of the earth. If we are self-centered and if we ignore the laws of nature, we build up negative energy fields and weaken our state of balance and that of the earth.

In the middle of June 2016, I met a Yoga student during a walk. In our conversation, he told me about the book series «Anastasia», written by Vladimir Megre. In the following days, he came to the center and lent me the first book. When I started reading the book, I found a text passage that describes exactly and in detail, how our state of consciousness co-creates what happens on earth.

«Only the light of a human being radiates in the cosmos, and from the cosmos, only beneficial radiations reach the earth. From a man with an evil mind, a dark radiation emanates, which cannot ascend. The energy enters the interior of the earth. From there thrown back, it returns to the surface, in the form of volcanic eruptions, earthquakes, and wars» (Megre, 2013, p.22)

From the point of view of the Earth, every environmental disaster is an attempt to liberate itself from an excess of negative energies. This is comparable to a disease that a person can get if he carries too much disharmonic energy within. Then the body causes a more or less heavy symptomatic reaction that is created to help the person to release the negative energies out of his system and to return itself to its original equilibrium. The same principle can be applied to the earth. The only difference is that when the Earth responds, humanity will be affected and the consequences for every individual will be of greater magnitude.

When we look around the world, it becomes clear that most people are not in harmony with themselves, and that they carry strong emotional and mental imbalances. Amongst other things, they result mainly from karma, samskaras, but also from external energetic influences like artificially generated energy frequencies, or occupations by negative entities. All the problems we face in our lives are the result of these imbalances. They are an expression of the Kali Yuga and our separation from the divine source.

If you believe it or not, the unbalanced aspects in our interior are responsible for the current environmental catastrophes and wars. Because out of negative emotions and negative thought patterns no harmonic and peaceful actions can follow. Because the majority of people carry many energetic imbalances within them, they generate and strengthen the negative forces in nature. Because negative emotions and negative thought-structures create discordant negative energy fields, which we radiate into nature and which burden the energetic overall balance of the earth. In addition, they man cannot follow harmonic and peaceful actions. Currently, there is a veil of various negative energies over the entire earth. If we don´t dissolve it in time, great challenges are going to come for humanity. Because these imbalances contribute significantly to the fact that the equilibrium of the earth is almost close to collapse. We are highly encouraged to overcome our inner imbalances through inner work. This is necessary to stabilize energetic field of the earth and to increase the lightful forces in nature.

From the perspective of nature, it is certain that the golden age will come, and that the earth will clean itself before elevating the energy frequency to the level of Satya Yuga. Achieving the energy frequency is a necessary prerequisite to move into the Satya Yuga.

How intensively the purification process will finally manifest on the physical level, meaning if it will be gentle or heavy, will depend on how much we do dissolve the negative energies in us and nature now. At the moment, a veil of negativity is covering the whole earth.

If we restore the energetic balance by increasing the light on earth and ourselves before the three-day purification process will start, then we will stabilize the balance of the earth and we can make it possible, that the transition into the new age will be more gentle and major catastrophes will not happen.

The entire work of the 19 Siddhas is based on providing human beings and the earth with all instruments and support from the highest frequency level, that are needed to help humanity and the earth find their energetic balance, as quickly as possible and to come into harmony with the high vibration frequency of the soul.

Highest frequency in this context means, that all methods and tools that are given are charged with the highest divine light and will elevate us and our environment energetically to the level of the Satya Yuga. The high frequencies superimpose themselves over the lower ones of the Kali Yuga. Furthermore, the soul frequency of a human being is getting activated, whereby a person can awaken to his true light and life more quickly.

The work of the 19 Siddhas is based, amongst other things, on divine alchemy. The 19 Siddhas were not only yogis and doctors but also alchemists. Alchemy is an ancient science that existed in all ancient cultures and mystical schools. Through alchemy, it becomes possible that high-frequency divine light is brought into the matter and the matter can be energetically transformed. This becomes possible because matter does not really exist.

The physicist and inventor Nicola Tesla expressed it in this way: if we want to understand how the Universe works, we should learn to think in terms of energy, vibrations, and frequencies. In nature, there exist countless forms of energies which vibrate at different frequencies. According to Einstein, matter is nothing more than vibration, which has been reduced in such a way, that it becomes perceptible to the five senses. Spirit shapes matter. We observe it in creative creating processes, like building a house or painting a picture.

Through the work of the 19 Siddhas, we are given the medicine and the opportunity to make the necessary energetic transformation processes, on the inner and outer level, in harmony with the current processes of nature. They give us the necessary and powerful medicine to correct errors in nature that man has created and to dissolve and free the internal and the external nature from all disharmonic energy frequencies, which man has created in nature and which do not correspond to the Satya Yuga. Thereby they help to bring us and the earth into its original energetic equilibrium. The more energetic equilibrium there is on earth, the gentler the transition to the new age.

The Divine works through different people as its mediators to prepare the process of ascension and transformation on Earth. An important mediator of the 19 Siddhas is Sriraman. Sriraman is one of the closest disciples of Sri La Sri Mahananda Siddha and Agastya Rishi. For more than 15 years, each of his steps has been guided by Agastya Rishi.

Over the last 15 years, the Divine Mother, the 19 Siddhas and other masters have blessed him with many abilities, tasks, and instruments to help people and the earth in the current transformation process, to liberate themselves from the energetic encounter forces of the Kali Yuga, and to activate the light of the soul. Since 2011, he has received all alchemical remedies from Agastya.

A BLESSING AND WARNING AT THE SAME TIME

In the spiritual world, the love and grace for mankind are very big. It is the desire of the Divine that as many people as possible are able to make the ascent. It wants to protect us and to prevent us from the great catastrophes so that the transition becomes gentle and free from lots of pain.

Until the last moment, we have all support we need from the spiritual world, to be able to avert the potentially threatening events.

But we must understand that we must overcome ignorance and work together with nature.

We are doing well to abandon all ignorance and to work with nature and accept its offer, even when it may not correspond to the kind of ideas we have had of spirituality so far.

However, we have to understand, that the ascent process and the related developmental possibilities of these times, as they are currently available to us, have a time limit. The divine creativity can't be pressed into ideas and imaginations.

It is much more challenging to search for the right understanding and to move that perspective forward than to withdraw into the security of the old thinking habits. Furthermore, the laws of the soul-consciousness cannot be understood by the ego-perspective. As long as we believe we know everything better, we are prisoners of our ego. We are called upon to develop a greater understanding of the connections in nature.

It is also important to understand that from the karmic point of view, humanity has currently a kind of open account with nature, that we have not balanced until now. We, humans, have caused the current state on earth by exploiting the earth and creating negative disharmonic energy fields. For many decades we have lived in a one-sided relationship with the earth. We lived at the expense of other creatures, have taken more than we should have, only to satisfy our over-selfish wants. Our behavior towards Mother Earth has caused great energetic imbalances and damage. Nature always strives to come back to energetic balance and harmony. This is necessary so that the energetic balance and harmony in the universe can be maintained. Now, it is our turn as humans to act and to help the earth to return to its energetic equilibrium by becoming active, changing our behavior towards creation, and getting into our energetic balance, as well as helping the earth to come into its own too. A wonderful and unique possibility and invitation to make that happen is the work of the 19 Siddhas.

The work of each individual counts and will decide how intensively the purification process will ultimately manifest itself onto the physical level. Everyone who is willing to take responsibility and participates will be a blessing on earth and for mankind. On the one hand it is a joyful and hopeful message, but on the other hand, also an urgent one. Because there is not much time left! The salvation of the earth should be a priority for all people. It will be our own at the same time.

WHAT IS MAHA POORNA ATMA YOGA?

An important energetic instrument for the purification of our consciousness that was transmitted by Agastya through the Palm Leaf library is called «Maha Poorna Atma Yoga». Maha Poorna Atma Yoga means «Great Cleansing of the Soul».

Maha Poorna Atma Yoga is a purification frequency and a simple practice that gradually initiates a process of cleaning of the subconscious mind. By practicing Maha Poorna Atma Yoga, the energetic charge on potential reaction patterns, like anger, shame, guilt, fear, and other destructive emotions in the subconscious will be transformed step by step. This helps humanity to develop inner peace more easily. To be in inner peace will be crucial for the coming time.

Through the purification process, the consciousness comes back into the present. This enables a permanent access to the natural inner knowledge of the soul and its power. This leads to harmonious actions in life that are in harmony with nature. To follow the impulses of the soul brings fulfillment and happiness.

Through the Palm-Leaf library, Agastya Rishi said that by practicing Maha Poorna Atma Yoga, the light in the individual and collective consciousness will rapidly rise. The more people, who sincerely practice Maha Poorna Atma Yoga, the more their own energetic balance, and that of the Earth, will be strengthened.

In an initiation by persons authorized by Agastya, the energy frequency of Maha Poorna Atma Yoga will be activated in the energy field of a person. After the initiation, the initiated person receives a kind of prayer, with which they continue to practice on their own, and it activates the purification frequency. Nature then starts working with the person.

The practice of Maha Poorna Atma Yoga is very universal, independent from religion and suitable for EVERYONE, without any special pre-knowledge. For more information and experiential reports about Maha Poorna Atma Yoga, visit the Homepage:

www.maha-poorna-atma-yoga.com

NEW ENERGY WORLD

I would like to use this book as a medium to present «NEW ENERGY WORLD» and to make the important background information available to all readers.

When I was in India for the first time in October of 2013, I received the message from Agastya to work for NEW ENERGY WORLD. At this time I was not yet able to recognize the profound meaning behind that. I only had a limited understanding and I was also a great critic. However, at that time I already felt that NEW ENERGY WORLD would be of great importance for Earth and humankind. That was the reason why I decided to work for it and to trust that the right knowledge will be revealed to me, at the right time.

During my stay in India, we were working on the development of the «MAHA-AURA CARD», which contains an alchemical formula that neutralizes various negative energy frequencies that affect the human energy field from outside, such as, electrosmog and water veins.

When I returned from India to Germany in February 2014, I visited an aunt and an uncle of mine. Until a few years ago, my aunt worked as a naturopath. Together with my uncle, they had developed a procedure which allowed them to record the health condition of a patient within a very short time. Her practice was very successful.

On one day during my visit, they gave me an insight into their work. I had physical symptoms for about half a year which I had not known before. Whenever I practiced certain breathing exercises of yoga or stepped up and down stairs, I got problems with my breathing. I was short-winded. Probably I would have never found out by myself that I had an inflammation of my heart muscle. This was caused by a virus that had been transmitted by a tick bite. In a later message from the Palm Leaf library, Agastya confirmed the diagnosis of my aunt. This message proved to my inner critic that their procedure really worked.

I was already surprised on my arrival how much my aunt and my uncle were dealing with the electrosmog issue. Everywhere in their house, all of the equipment that the market had to offer to protect it against electrosmog, was in place. «By causality» I had a Maha-Aura- Card with me. I wanted to know what my uncle said about this card. I asked him if we could test the card with his procedure. He agreed and so we did some tests. The results astonished me deeply.

First, we found out that the card charges the human energy field with energy and protects it within the radius of one meter against outer negative energetic influences. These include natural imbalances like water veins, Curry grids, etc., but also man-made artificial energy frequencies too, like mobile funk. We were also able to figure out that negative energies are neutralized and harmonized by the card and that the environment got transformed energetically into a bright place within a certain radius. Furthermore, we were able to measure that the card does not generate any energy side-effects (comparable to unwanted side-effects) and that it works one hundred percent in harmony with nature. According to a message from Agastya, this card can do even more.

In addition to the MAHA AURA, there exist now also other developments that are responding to and transforming the complexity of the energetic level.

According to the tests we made and in combination with the knowledge I received later on, I gradually began to understand the great blessing of NEW ENERGY WORLD. The alchemical remedies of Agastya give mankind the chance to correct the misprocesses that we have created in nature and to raise the energy frequency to that of Satya Yuga. Because we, as human beings, are no longer able to correct them by our own efforts, we receive divine help.

Through the alchemical formulas, we can heal the energy level and can transform our environment into energetically high-frequency places that correspond to the Satya Yuga. This will strengthen and stabilize the balance of the earth and will allow a smooth transition into the new age. It is up to us if we take this opportunity and accept this extraordinary offer, or if we think we have greater knowledge and greater wisdom than the Divine, and so reject this offer.

In 2015, our team received the message from Agastya that the spreading of the alchemical remedies will be held back because mankind is still not ready to receive them. As soon as the spreading is allowed, they will be available, incorporated into everyday products. The homepage is: **www.new-energy-world.org**

MAHANANDHA SIDDHA AND SRIRAMAN

Chapter 5

The new cosmic man

The consciousness of the coming Golden Age will be shaped by unity. Man will live with his soul, his fellows, the earth and the laws of nature in harmony, respect, peace, and love. There will be no separation between nationalities and religions. Mankind becomes ONE nation. Until we get there, we have some work to do. At first, we are called upon to make an inner and outer transformation. Nothing that is not in love and peace can exist in the future. It will break apart or it will turn against us. We are called upon to lead everything into love. What are the virtues of the new human being and what do we have to develop, to become a human being of the New Age? How can mankind create their outer life to come into harmony with nature? In this chapter, we will deal with this question for the inner orientation.

THE CONSCIOUS CREATOR

In Satya Yuga, the golden age, the higher spiritual powers such as telepathy, clairvoyance, etc. are fully awakened. This means, that our thoughts, which are the basis of our creations, will be realized much more quickly into manifestation than they have done up to now. Because a higher vibration frequency of a human being means that thoughts and emotions become more spontaneous, and manifest themselves much more quickly. That is why it will be important that we learn to deal with our thoughts and emotions through inner work. If we stay centered and not get involved in our emotionality and our thought carousel, our mind becomes clear and our life energy flows more easily.

A clear mind will help us to feel our inner essence consciously and to decide consciously if we follow the impulses of the ego or the creative impulses of the soul. This ability corresponds to the conscious creator.

People, whose consciousness is still strongly in the third dimension, are not aware that they are the creators of their own reality. Because of past injuries, they still react from the impulses of their injured ego and repeat the old dramas in the present time again and again. Every time we react in the old, familiar way, we recharge the old reaction patterns with energy, and so intensify the energetic binding to our circles of suffering.

Many people do not know that they cannot be non-creators. We manifest our reality continuously, 24 hours a day, consciously or unconsciously. What kind of reality we create in the outer world essentially depends on, if we follow the impulses of the ego or those of the soul.

Many people are insecure about how these two impulses can be distinguished from each other. The distinction is actually quite simple. Impulses coming from the ego are reactive and often associated with strong emotionality. They are based on a personal egocentric perspective, such as demands and expectations. If we follow them, they lead to blockages of the life energy flow and lower the frequency of our consciousness. Impulses coming from the soul are marked by love, compassion, and peace. They lead to transformation and the expansion of consciousness. They connect us with our creative potential.

The soul communicates through feelings, not through emotions. This distinction is important. While emotions disturb the inside, feelings that come from the soul arise in a peaceful and calm state of mind.

The conscious versus the unconscious creator

People whose consciousness is still strongly anchored on the third dimension of consciousness who have the perpetrator-victim consciousness are not aware that they are creators of their own reality. Because of past, not overcome injuries, they react from the impulses of their injured ego and repeat the old dramas in the present over and over again. Every time we react in the old familiar way, we energize the old reaction patterns and increase the energetic attachment to the cycles of suffering.

An unconscious creator is not aware of a difference between ego and soul consciousness. Therefore he doesn't know that he can follow different impulses from within, to determine his reality. He also does not understand that the following of these two different types of impulses cause different consequences in his life.

Everyone can become a conscious creator. We can train this by trial and error. The first step on in this path is to learn self-observation and to differentiate between the thoughts, emotions, feelings, and actions of the soul, and those of the ego. If we have acted in a certain way, we can learn to feel if the situation created an opening and blissful feeling or if it has triggered us and created a cramped feeling inside us. Narrow emotions come from the ego, inner width is created by the soul.

The second step on this path is to realize that we are the one who creates our reality, one hundred percent. It happens anyway, whether we are conscious or unconscious of it. We ourselves are solely responsible for our decisions on which impulses we follow from within, and how we deal with internal and external situations. Through this, we can realize that we ourselves are the ones who can change the reality by changing the situation or perspective.

Projections as a mirror of self-knowledge

An important instrument on the journey to a conscious creator and self-knowledge is the outside world. In every situation, we are mirrors for others and mirrored at the same time. The unconscious creator experiences himself as a victim of his circumstances. He projects his inner to the outside world and makes others responsible for his suffering and well-being. The conscious creator learns to use projections as an instrument of self-knowledge. He is aware that the source of peace, understanding, love, harmony, and happiness lies within him, and that there is something to correct in himself when he suffers and doesn´t experience one of these qualities.

If we observe our projections of other people, we gradually develop the ability to realize more and more in which situations, and how, we blame other people for our inner experiences. For example, if we experience rejection, we take responsibility for our inner state and ask ourselves: how did I create this situation in my life? Where do I perhaps reject myself? What is my part, what is the part of the other in this situation? Am I in love with myself, and my opposite? Through practice, we get more and more to know ourselves and learn to differentiate more quickly.

Patterns of faith are unconscious choices

If we understand how we process life experiences through our subtle energy bodies, we can increase the mindfulness in our self-realizing process.

Through our five sense organs, we take experiences in the form of information into our system. Within milliseconds, the incoming information is compared with stored information in the subconscious in a kind of search process. If one of these incoming pieces of information resonates with a stored one, it starts vibrating energetically, and the emotions and thought patterns which are associated with it are activated. Then the emotions and thought pattern rise as energy waves into our consciousness and cause an effect. If our «inner buttons» are triggered and issues that are emotionally charged are touched, like restlessness, anger, fear, envy, jealousy, etc., we connect to these emotions and a reaction chain starts in our consciousness. The originally calm and observing consciousness mixes up with the irritated emotional energy. In that moment we lose our neutrality towards a situation and distort it through our injured thoughts and feelings. These distortions contain the potential that we react to the situation with inadequate and disharmonic reaction patterns.

At this point, our intuition that leads us from within gets distorted, and we lose our state of inner clarity. There are many people who have never experienced the inner observer throughout their whole lifetime because their mental activity is always moving. Therefore, they believe that reactive thinking and behavior is normal.

If we remain unconscious of our creations, we will become repeat offenders, bound by our reactions, and will maintain or intensify the conflicts. Man is bound to these conflicts until he is ready to change his perspective. Often we are prompted by crises to make a correction and give our life a new direction. Many people only change their inner, when the inner pain has become intensive enough. Seen from this perspective, pain is a great blessing. It prevents us getting stuck in old thought and behaviors patterns, and throws us out of our comfort zones.

Basically, our old reaction patterns are only solutions that we used unconsciously, to deal with certain life experiences. Many of these solutions we have learned in our childhood. At that time they were often necessary to protect us from pain. The problem is that we are still using them in the present, even if they are inadequate to a situation. If we react to situations inappropriately, we invite conflicts into our lives. The good news is that we can change our perspectives and learn to deal more harmoniously with situations. An example will make clear what is meant:

During her childhood, Marie often heard from her father that he had preferred a baby boy to be born. Because of his unfulfilled wish and dissatisfaction, he often made Marie humbled and verbally humiliated. These situations were traumatic for Marie. They burned themselves emotionally and mentally deeply into her subconscious, in the form of negative beliefs about herself. One of her unconscious beliefs is, «I am not worthy of being loved» Because of this belief, she was very shy as a child and has avoided contact with other people. Her fear was that she could be hurt and rejected.

As an adult woman, it is still a torment for her to be in social contact. In exchanges with other people, she feels quickly rejected and unloved. This always leads her to further isolation and to be unhappy.

One day, Marie realizes she does not want to live like this. She wants to change something about her situation. She can see how quickly she feels rejected and sees the associated fears and self-insecurities. But she knows that she needs inspiration and help to get out of her situation.

In a library, she finds an inspiring book where she gets valuable advice on how to overcome her shyness and anxiety. In addition, she finds a loving therapist who helps her, as a good counterpart for changing the perspective regarding herself. Over time, she learns to accept and love herself more. With a lot of patience, the first successes become apparent after some time. She finds a girlfriend with whom she starts to meet regularly.

Our wrong beliefs we have mostly taken on, from our parents, but also by a school system, which often does not correspond to our inner truth. Many people believe unconditionally what they have been taught and create their lives from these conditioned perspectives. For example, if I follow unconsciously the belief that I am not lovable, I will always create situations in my life which correspond to this belief and will confirm it.

To become a conscious creator, we need a third key through which we are able to change our belief patterns, into a more harmonious perspective that is in harmony with our soul and the divine wisdom in us.

We should understand that our belief system has been manifested by unconscious decision-making processes. Especially in our childhood and in school, we have decided unconsciously to believe in negative perspectives, in relation to ourselves and life. These unconscious subtle decisions from our childhood continue to influence us into adulthood. They do so until we realize how they limit our being. Then, after a long time of suffering, we have finally had enough. We begin to look behind the facades and recognize and reveal all the untruths and half-truths that have imprisoned us. We begin to free ourselves from the narrowness and to look at life from a higher and truer perspective.

Once we have understood that we are the ones who can injure or heal ourselves with the choice of our thoughts, then the change in our perspective on life becomes faster, lighter and more playful over time. We recognize that we can exchange thoughts and can create a new reality. Increasingly, we begin to identify with the positive creative thoughts and feelings of the soul. We make choices based on love, joy, peace, forgiveness, and harmony.

If we have a lack of ideas about how we can deal with a situation in a more salutary and harmonious way, we can get inspiration, for example, from books, participating in seminars or taking other people as role models that have already developed the quality that we want to develop. There are no limits to creativity in our learning process.

At this point, the right treatment of emotions should be clarified also, so that we are able to maintain the clarity of our consciousness continuously. Emotions are generated by thoughts. If they emerge, they are there and we cannot simply push them back into our subconscious minds. Because if we do that, they act like a radioactive waste that still radiates, and they cost us repression energy and thus life energy. It is important to let rise up the energy of the emotions into our consciousness, to allow us to feel them and finally to accept them lovingly. If we are able to remain uninvolved and to stay in the inner observation, the clear consciousness remains unaffected. The reaction chains that result from a mixture of consciousness, thoughts, and emotions are not amplified. In this way, we allow the emotions to flow through us and to dissolve.

Three levels of manifestation in the process of creation

In our creating process, there are three levels of creation through which we manifest our reality. These three levels are thought, word and action. If we become aware of this, we can further differentiate our inner experiences through observation and consciousness.

The most subtle forms of our creation process are our thoughts. Everything we can see in the external world is actually a visible thought. Energy shapes matter. For example, every house built by an architect was created by creative thoughts.

The quality of our thoughts plays a decisive role in which reality we manifest. Thoughts can be either selfish or soul-motivated. Thoughts that originate in the ego are narrow in their perspective, self-centered and accompanied by emotions such as anger, jealousy, inferiority, envy, pleasure-satisfaction, etc. Thoughts that spring from the soul are non-binding, selfless, loving, inspiring, unconditional, compassionate, peaceful, joyful and creative.

Through our words and actions, our intentions become visible in the external world. In that our actions have the strongest expressive power. They also lead to the greatest consequences: positive and negative. If a person strives to take another's life only in thoughts, this will have no consequences in the outside world. If he brings these thoughts into action and he kills someone, he will become a murderer and has to go to prison if caught. In the positive sense, if someone thinks of helping hungry children and will manifest these thoughts, he will be able to save the lives of many people and will change their lives for the better. If these thoughts stay without action, there will be no positive change on the outside.

We can change the process of creation

On all levels of creation, we have the opportunity to become self-aware of ourselves, and to change the process of manifestation into a more favorable direction. This is important, especially if we have mainly followed the impulses of the ego before. For example, if we realize our negative ego-motivated thought patterns at the right time, we can prevent manifesting them in the external world, by not saying words and taking actions that hurt others.

In my opinion, a very effective way to change behavioral and thought patterns is a method presented by Neale Donald Walsh in his book, «Conversation with God.» According to this, we can simply reverse the creation process. On a mental level, we develop a kind of vision or idea of how we want to react to a particular situation in the future. We paint an inner picture in detail of how we would think, feel and act if we have already developed this new pattern. In a next step, we nurture this vision with energy by speaking and acting in the outer world as if we had already developed the new behavior a long time ago. As a result, we enter a new area of experience in the interior and exterior world. If we experience more and more that our new behavior leads to success and brings more joy, harmony, and love to us and others, we are encouraged to leave the old tracks and enter a new path. At the beginning, this method requires some patience and discipline. At first, you can have a feeling of not being authentic. This feeling will disappear when you realize that the method works and leads to the desired changes.

Healing of the Female Energy

Each person carries female (yin) and male (yang) energies within themselves. The feminine energy stands for qualities like pure being, resting in oneself, emptiness, healing, relaxation, intuition, care, spirituality and mysticism. The male energy stands for consciousness, rationality, goal-directedness, independence, and action. A woman carries a higher proportion of the female energy in her consciousness. A man has a higher proportion of male energy. To be able to live a balanced and holistic life, the harmony and integration of both energies in our consciousness are needed.

In the last centuries, the male energy mainly dominated the life on earth. This is evident even today and is visible through the suppression of women. This suppression took place in the past and is still taking place all over the world. Women have been, and still are, partially regarded as a possession of the man, and still suffer a lot. This has been caused by the power of the church and other religions, which have feared and demonized the feminine qualities. They should have been eradicated by witch burnings in Christianity, for example.

With emancipation in the 1970´s, women in European countries started a movement that helped them to break out of the dominant male structures. This development had been of great importance and was necessary at that time. But what happened was that women orientated themselves to the values of the man. Instead of coming back to her original Yin essence and her real strength as a woman, she started to compete with the man and adapted herself to the man's yang energy.

This has not really liberated the women and didn´t bring her back to her original energetic equilibrium. To this day many women suppress their Yin essence and reject it. Many women feel an inner emptiness and a longing for something they often cannot describe. Amongst other things, it is the longing for her original female essence.

We, women, are asked to rediscover our original female power and to live it. Through this, we can become teachers of the female energy and qualities that are so urgently needed, for our own healing and that of the earth. The man, on the other hand, is called upon to enter his original male strength while at the same time integrating the female parts.

It is important to accept that men and women are different but overall are equal in their specific qualities. Through this, a healthy game of polar energies can revive in the man-woman relationship. In the new age, the male and the female energy will be in harmony.

THR WORK WITH THE INNER CHILD

The inner child in us represents an instance of consciousness, which is characterized on the one hand, by playfulness, spontaneity, creativity, the joy of life and emotionality and on the other hand also by the injuries of the past.

Children want to be loved and accepted unconditionally and to express themselves freely in their creativity and originality. But to live that in our kind of society is not easy. Many generations before us have not been able to live their originality and have been shaped by a social morality that has been transferred from generation to generation for centuries. There was a lack of role models that would have given us an idea of how we can live it. We cannot and should not blame our parents because of this. They did not know it well as we do now and would of course have done it much better if they had known how to live it.

It is the inner work of the current generation, to reveal the untruth, to correct all wrong beliefs, to free oneself from mind-constructed morals, and to come back to our own originality.

For the healing process, it may be important to understand the dynamics that have been developed by morality and oppression in us.

As already mentioned, every child longs for love. Unconditional love is the food that keeps the child alive. Most of us have experienced a lack of love during our childhood and have had traumatic experiences through lovelessness. In this way, we have experienced fundamental injuries that have deeply buried themselves in our subconscious. Through the experience of a lack of love, many people are needy and have developed a demanding part inside themselves, for love and recognition. These needy parts in us are not a good basis for a relationship. If we do not heal it, it will affect us until our whole life, and it creates dependencies in our relationships. Because we are not nourished inwardly, we believe we have to look for it on the outside.

Unfortunately, through disappointments in relationships, we have to keep reminding ourselves that the needy parts in us are not a good basis for a relationship, and the relationship must fail long-term if we do not cure them. We have to learn that we cannot blame others for our own happiness, but we must seek it in ourselves. And that's good. We are prompted to heal all the injured emotions, inferiority, guilt and shame caused by this deficiency within us, and to find the source of love in ourselves.

Love is to give and not to take. The injured inner child demands love and has to struggle with strong feelings of inferiority. The healed inner child is giving itself away in love. Once we have completed this development, we are able to nourish ourselves and become free creative beings.

In the last centuries, many of the beautiful talents that were brought into life by the healed and creative inner child remained inanimate and were not expressed to the world to make it more colorful and joyful. We have now arrived at a time when we are urgently invited to discover our talents and to unfold them and to enrich the world through them.

Parents of the next generation are being asked for a new form of education. An upbringing that does not impose something from the outside on the child, but which allows it´s inner nature to come up in a natural and loving way. The healing and integration of the inner child lead us to vitality, integrity, and authenticity and is of great importance in our time. The current world is full of injured children, which prevents the world from finding peace.

DETACHMENT

All of our inner states of suffering are basically based on attachment. The inner holds onto something and can´t allow the flow of being to happen. We can be attached to feelings, thoughts, sexuality, money, image, fear, injuries, habits, people, etc.

Attachments cause suffering if we react either with resistance or with desire. If we ward off a particular situation and if we do not accept the feelings and thoughts that are associated with it, the fights in us will continue. If we react with desire, we want to repeat an experience that has produced pleasant feelings in us. The stronger the inner struggle or the desire, the stronger we are bound to the conflict and the more intense is our suffering.

A key feature of energy is that it wants to flow. There is a kind of natural flow of life that begins to run when we are centered in ourselves. It feels like as if we are being carried effortlessly by life, from event to event. But as soon as we cling to something, the flow of energy stops and energetic blockages build up.

Many people partly cling to circumstances, ideas or other people for decades, even when they no longer serve their inner development and do not correspond to their deep inner truth. In this way, their creative life energy is frozen and they feel unhappy.

Everyone can learn to release attachments. The first step is to realize them. We can recognize them when we feel that we suffer. If we suffer, we are not in harmony with ourselves. Something inside us holds onto expectations or thought patterns, which creates a pain-causing condition. Actually, we mainly suffer from thoughts that arise and we do not accept. Because of them we feel disturbed and suffer.

The paradox is that the desired change often occurs when we change our thinking and find acceptance in our situation. Accepting of what is, does not mean that we become inactive and accept everything. It means to give our best to improve our inner situation, but at the same time not to be frustrated if that what we wish for is not happening at the present time.

Most people are afraid of change. This is one of the main reasons that they cling to external circumstances. Change is a solid and natural part of life. It will happen if we want it to or not. If something is for sure in this world, then it is that nothing will remain as it is now. Experiences and people will come and go. The current state of life will change either gradually or suddenly. If we become aware of the fear behind this reality, we can transform it.

Accepting change is the key to liberating our lives from attachments. If we accept changes, we give the inner force the freedom to control our lives. We flow and respond to that that is. We allow a higher power to guide us that has greater wisdom and greater knowledge than ourselves. That leads us to relax into our own lives, to trust life and enjoy what is right now without getting stuck to it.

In this process, we are given the chance to learn that nothing in our lives is normal and that nothing belongs to us. Everything that comes into our life is like a lending. It remains for a while and will go again, by separation during our lifetime or by death. If we learn to accept this natural process of nature and flow with it, we begin to enjoy the present moment and be grateful for what is Now. Then when the day of farewell comes, because a cycle ends, we are ready to let go and to release ourselves into a new life, in an attitude of gratitude and recognition for all that what was and is.

THE INNER OBSERVER

The «inner observer» is a special space of experience within a human being. With the help of the inner observer, we can learn to observe the constantly changing mental and emotional inner movements, like a distant observer watching a film. The inner observer is especially important when it comes to distinguishing between ego and soul consciousness and to recognize and change thought and behavioral patterns.

On the level of energy, our destructive and often unconscious reaction patterns are comparable with wood pieces that we throw into a burning fire. By reacting in the same way, again and again, we feed the energy of the fire. In this way, we keep it burning. Only when we learn to rest in the inner observer and cease to respond in the old way, then we stop throwing wood into it and withdraw our energy from it. Finally, it expires.

The secret to dissolve old reaction patterns and wounds is to allow their energy to rise up into our consciousness but to remain untouched and quiet at the same time. They rise. We watch them. We feel them. We just let them be there without oppressing or rejecting them and choose consciously not to respond to our destructive habits. We stay undisturbed. We don´t react. Because we know if we follow the destructive impulses of the ego, we create disharmony within ourselves and in our interpersonal relationships. If we stand firm and stop feeding the old dramas with energy, they become weaker and dissolve at some point.

In this context, the inner observer intervenes between the situation and the automatic reaction. In the interior of a person, it creates a temporal and spatial distance through which we are given the opportunity to view and reflect our thinking and reaction patterns, from a distance. This allows us to realize them. We get the liberty to choose our reactions and perspectives on experiences consciously. That means we decide if we want to repeat the old dramas again and again or if we choose a more healing and harmonious reaction. The inner observer can be strengthened by mindfulness and meditation.

On our way to more harmonious reactions, we may initially revert to old patterns and move between destructive and constructive patterns for some time. This is normal and belongs to the learning process. Any relapse is actually an advance because it gives us important insights about ourselves and our reactions. Through relapses, we become spiritually stronger. We learn to resist the opposing forces from the inside in a better way. We are also developing more and more distinctiveness, which helps us to transform unconsciousness into consciousness and ignorance into knowledge and wisdom. It is important not to give up and to continue to practice consistently and patiently. The day will come when we have mastered all destructive parts within ourselves and thus gained the mastery over ourselves.

The neutral Perspective

The neutral perspective arises when we rest in the inner observer. It is free of judgment and exists beyond polarity. From the neutral point of view, we are pure being, relaxed in ourselves, not evaluating, but observing, peaceful, perceptive, and accepting in relation to what is. It is the third point of view which arises when we are in equilibrium.

Out of it, we look with equanimity at our experiences. Our consciousness remains undisturbed by the movements of inner and outer life. Finally, it is the judging mind which evaluates experiences and divides them into positive and negative. It causes a firework of emotional and mental movement.

The neutral standpoint exists beyond mental and emotional activity. From that point of view, every experience we make in life is perfect as it is. It does not matter if it is pleasant or unpleasant. From its point of view, there is only the pure experience and the related lessons. The purpose of experiences is to lead the individual soul to more maturity, growth, knowledge, and wisdom.

The neutral position is an optimist. It is full of wisdom. It knows that in the end, everything will always be good, no matter what experience we have gone through before. It knows that experiences are only made for us to grow. The neutral standpoint is the divine standpoint at the same time.

Beyond Good and Evil

Everyone has experienced uncomfortable situations in his life, which seemed to him bad at first, but turned out to be a blessing in the future. For example, a dispute that we have had with someone, and which we feel subjectively at first terrible, can lead to greater proximity, growth, and connectedness in the relationship, through the power of clarification and forgiveness. Or we did not get what we wanted at a certain point in time, and only later we realize how good it was for us that we didn´t get it.

If we live in the understanding that also unpleasant experiences contain a lot of abundances, then we are ready to accept them. We can stay peaceful and draw positive conclusions from them. We trust that it has its purpose why we experience such situations, even if the meaning is not clear to us at a certain point in time.

I would like to share a story, which I once heard in a wonderful Satsang given by the wonderful Mooji, on a YouTube video. From the neutral point of view it illustrates how unpleasant experiences can turn into a blessing:

The story of the rider

A king lives in his castle and loves riding. One day he falls off his horse and breaks his arm. That means he can´t ride. He calls his counselor, laments and asks him about the reason for the accident. In this situation, the counselor gives an answer to the king that the king doesn´t accept. So it comes that in his anger he puts the counselor in the dungeon.

One day, the king cannot stand it anymore, to be in the situation in which he is condemned to inactivity. He misses the riding and the feeling of liberty that he is associating with it. And so he goes beyond his safe limits. He climbs his horse despite his broken arm, and rides out, over fields, meadows, and forests. He rides on and on to an unknown area.

Suddenly he is stopped by a horde of wild men. They obstruct his way, encircle him and threaten him with spears. They take the king and his horse and imprison the king in a cage in their village. There he is kept captive for days. During this time he gets to know that he is intended to be a sacrificial meal for one of their gods. The king looks anxiously towards the end of his days.

Then the day of the sacrifice arrives. The people are preparing for the ceremony. The fire is kindled, the drums begin to beat. The cage is opened and the struggling king is carried towards the fire. In this situation, the sleeve of his shirt slips up slightly. Suddenly, the drums stop beating. Silence! The chief pulls the king's shirt sleeve all the way up and sees the broken arm. In the folk, there is a loud moaning. Because of the broken arm, they can´t sacrifice him. The sacrifice for their divinity must be perfect.

So they let him go. They fetch the king's horse, saddle it, and raise the king. They give the horse a strong slap on the butt and it runs off, in the forest, over fields and meadows, back to the castle. There, the king needs to recover for a few days from his horror trip.

After some days, he remembers his poor adviser, who is still in prison. The king releases him and is full of repentance. He apologizes to him and says, «Oh dear counselor, how could I do this to you? You are always faithfully by my side and surrendered to me, and I have given you such a terrible experience because of anger about my broken arm. Will you ever forgive me?»

Thereupon the counselor smiles wise and replies: «Dear King, I am your counselor, and always faithful to you. Where you are, I am also. Where would I be now if you had not put me in the dungeon?»

Sometimes intensive experiences are of great importance in life so that the crusts of the ego can break up. Our egoism and injuries can become visible sometimes only under very specific conditions and experiences. Through intense situations, we get the opportunity to become aware of our blind spots and to develop more kindness and love.

Once we have learned our lessons, we have neutralized them according to our emotions and reactions. We have transformed the subject into the neutral perspective. The issue will no longer affect us emotionally in the future.

INNER PEACE

Most people are in a state of war inwardly. They carry many disharmonies in themselves and are constantly in conflict with themselves and other people. Inner peace is important so that we can experience happiness, abundance, contentment, and harmony in our lives, regardless of the circumstances that surround us. Inner peace results from the neutral point of view, when we have learned to rest permanently in it.

It arises when expectations towards people and situations have completely disappeared from us and we have finished our internal struggles. This includes the fact that, despite all the challenges and pleasant and unpleasant life experiences we have made, we have learned to love and to accept our life unconditionally, with everything that belongs to it: mistakes, pleasures, pleasant and unpleasant feelings and thoughts.

Once we have achieved inner peace, the inner voice begins to speak to us. From this inner state, the flow of life begins to unfold in a beautiful way. We experience a tingling joy in our hearts. Life starts to carry us effortlessly from happening to happening in the most natural and easy way.

Experiences have a meaning

We don´t understand many of the experiences we make in our current lives. According to the circle of reincarnation, we have lived many lives. In different lives, we have made different life experiences, which affect the present life. Why we make certain experiences in the present life can be explained by the law of karma.

Karma means «action». The law of karma is an exact mathematical law of compensation, which means that everything we sow in the form of thoughts, actions, and desires will come back to us in the form of experiences one day: in both positive and negative directions. This preserves the energetic balance and harmony of the universe.

The seeds of our actions and desires we do not necessarily experience in the present life. Past life actions have an impact on the present life, and the present life will influence our future. Expressed in a simple way karma arises by positive and negative actions from motives that were not selfless. If we have injured others, we will be faced with a situation in the future in which we are also hurt. If we bring joy to others, joy will come back to us.

The universe records all our actions. There exists a kind of karma storage on the subtle energy level, in which all «open accounts» which we have with other people, ourselves (not living the purpose of our life) and of nature are being stored. This means for example, if we damage another human being and do not repair this damage, we will meet this being in one of the next lives again, to balance the bill or we will have a similar experience that will make us feel this same pain so that we can learn our lessons.

Open bills between two people and even groups may exist over several lives. The victim-perpetrator game only ends if one of the players gets out of the game and begins to act in love and forgiveness.

The karma storage is the reason why we are bound to the cycle of rebirth. Before we are born again, our soul chooses from this memory what it wants to experience, which means what kind of talents it will develop and what tasks it likes to do in the current life. This also includes which open bills we want to balance. According to this, we chose our family and the circumstances in which we are born.

Through birth into this life, a veil of oblivion is laid over us. This has been directed by nature so that we can get the best out of our chosen experiences and learn our lessons profoundly. Only at this point of understanding does it become clear how limited the human perspective is of our life experiences. Actually, only the divine consciousness itself and the self-realized spiritual master know the true reason why we make certain experiences in life.

Their perspective surpasses the one of a human and considers a being in front of the background of his past lives. Through the divine and the grace of a master, karmic accounts can be balanced without which a student has to go through experiences with all of their intensity.

There are people who claim to be their own guru. In the essence, this is true, but no master has fallen from heaven.

Achieving mastery is a path of development. In every discipline, no matter if we want to get mastery on a musical instrument or in a sport it is like this. Until we reach a certain level, we need teachers who have preceded us on the path, and who inspire and support us in our own development. At some point, we become masters of our own and continue to share our knowledge. This is also true for the spiritual path. Self-realization is not only an individual work. Indeed, on the one hand, it takes a readiness to self-realization and to listen to our own heart, but on the other hand, we also need the grace and guidance through the lightful powers, until we have fully developed our own guru.

Many people overlook the fact that without the divine grace we couldn´t walk on the spiritual way at all. If our will is strong enough to grow into our true being, then we are supported by the spiritual luminous forces from the background on all levels. They accompany and protect us. It can be possible that we are connected with a master in a special way from past lives. He or she can appear at a certain point on our path.

If we succeed in not opening up any new karmic accounts in our present life, the storage of karma begins to empty. For that inner peace is indispensable. The prerequisite for this is that our consciousness rests in inner peace and that we accept our life experiences with equanimity, neutrality and unconditionally. A soul who has learned all these lessons and balanced all open accounts becomes a free soul. In the future, she can decide freely whether she wants to incarnate on earth again or not.

How to cultivate inner peace

If we rest in inner peace, we accept ourselves and other people unconditionally. We cease to condemn ourselves and others for being as they are. We encounter all beings with love, respect, and understanding. According to this, we understand that our fellows, as well as ourselves, are suffering from the limitations of the ego. From this results compassion and from compassion, the understanding that we give up the injurious behavior towards other people, or not take it personally when someone tries to hurt us. Finally, we can only get hurt if we give permission to someone and to decide to feel hurt. Behind the hurtful and egoistic behavior of a person, often a deep, unconscious pain about the separation from the divine source becomes visible. If we understand this, then instead of counter-attack, we act out of an attitude of compassion, and we can think about how we can help others, as an instrument of love to overcome suffering.

The more we are anchored in inner peace, the more we learn to make our own mood independent of external situations and people, and to live permanently in our own true nature. We understand that only we ourselves are one hundred percent responsible for staying in inner peace in all situations, at all times.

How to develop inner peace? To be able to rest in it permanently, it is inevitable that we first strengthen the inner observer, for example through a regular meditation practice. It creates a healthy detachment to destructive thoughts and emotions in our inner being and saves us from entanglements with them.

There are many people who see themselves as a victim of fate. Over a long period of time, they are totally busy to find an answer to the question: «Why does it always happen to me?» This question leads at best to the fact that we stay in a worse situation instead of seeing the opportunities that arise to improve it. We would do better if we worked on constructive solutions that help us to liberate ourselves from our untoward situation. A constructive question, for example, is: «What can I learn? What possibilities do I have to change the situation?» If we go in search for these answers, our mind opens up to solutions and possibilities and begins to widen.

An excellent measuring instrument that shows us how far we have developed inner peace is how we respond to life experiences. The less we take the circumstances that surround us personally, and the more we remain untouched by them, the more we have cultivated inner peace within ourselves. Theoretically, this sounds easier than it is in practice. But through inner work and constant practice, we can realize this state.

Unconditional Love

Unconditional love and what is currently understood under the notion «love» in the most parts of the world are different forms of love. For this reason, first, a distinction must be made between unconditional love and conditioned love.

Conditional love is a self-centered form of love. It restricts the care and interest for other people and beings only to the nearer environment, like themselves, their partner, relatives, pets or close friends. In an open or concealed way, the love is connected to conditions, expectations, and demands. The conditional love is based on beliefs, like: «I have done this and that for you. Now it's your turn to do something for me.», «If I have sex with you, you will love me more.»

Conditional love is a kind of exchange business. Expectations, wishes, and ideas are projected onto other people and are expected to be fulfilled by them. If these remain unfulfilled, love is withdrawn.

Relations that are based on conditional love are not on an equal level. Through connoting feelings of guilt to others, but also by humiliating them, or increasing oneself, one's own self-esteem is defined and protected. Fears of bereavement, loneliness, and worthlessness are strong strangleholds and are responsible for the fact that people stay for years in dependent and unhappy relationships. In the end, both sides have something to learn. People who control or let themselves be controlled by others, have corresponding resonant fields and attract each other to learn from each other, and grow together.

If a person wishes to liberate himself from strangleholds of conditional love, this is often associated with some turbulence. Because systems based on dependencies fear changes. This can be seen, among other things, in verbal and physical attacks and can be accompanied by depreciation and condemnation, which are intended to prevent a person's liberation process. The motive behind is fear.

However, in unconditional love, relationships are based on freedom, appreciation, meekness, respect, and mindfulness. They are free from expectations and control mechanisms. We love because we know that we are the source of love. That is divine love. Encounters in unconditional love touch the heart and take place on the same level.

When we are anchored in unconditional love, enemies cease to exist. There is no longer any exclusion and no separation, even if there are temporary inconsistencies and different opinions according to how each person sees things. In our essence, we remain well-connected. We end the urge to want to be right. We tolerate that there are different truths and perspectives on one object, and allow them to exist side by side without judging them.

The unconditional love is universal and transcendental. It is the selfless giving of love and caring, without asking for anything in return. It includes the entire creation and is distributed to all living things in the same way. It also includes animals and plants. The unconditional love is like an invisible band that unites and holds everything together in the universe.

In a state of unconditional love, we have the deep desire that all beings are happy and that we contribute something to their happiness and well-being. We love every human being for what they are and accept him unconditionally in their So-Being without wanting to change them. If someone is strange or egoistic towards us, we try not to take it personally and also not to withdraw our love. We know that he shows this behavior because he has temporarily separated himself from the divine source and that it does not correspond to his true nature. In an attitude of compassion, we try to react with understanding and to be compassionate, forgiving, sympathetic and mild. A wonderful question whose answer can help us to overcome almost any difficult interpersonal situation in life is: «What would love do now?»

In this context, unconditional love does not mean that at the cost of our authenticity we always have to be nice and to endure everything. It means to represent our own truth in a nonviolent and gentle way and to respect the different truths of other people.

It is also important to mention self-love in this context. Only if we accept and love ourselves as we are, we are able to love others unconditionally too. Then we stop being beggars who lose ourselves in the search for recognition from the outside. Even Jesus emphasized the importance of self-love by saying, «love others as yourself.»

In this context, I would like to present an example from a film sequence of the film «Humans» by the filmmaker Yann Arthus-Bertrand. The film can be bought or viewed under the link listed in the bibliography at the end of this book.

In one of the first film sequences, there is shown a scene of a man who tells how unconditional love transformed his life. His story is a moving example of how transforming and powerful, the power of true love and forgiveness can be.

The man who is interviewed became a murderer in the past. He killed his former partner and her child. His biography shows that he himself was a victim of great violence in the past. During his childhood, he was mistreated by his stepfather. Because of his painful experiences, he developed false beliefs about what love is. For him, love was connected to how much pain others can carry caused by him. This unconscious association led him to commit the deed later.

What is truly touching in this story is that the mother and grandmother of the murdered daughter and granddaughter did not turn away from him, but went through a process of forgiveness. In spite of her deep pain, she was able to encounter him with compassion for his past. She stayed in contact with him and gave him the chance to repent and change. A greater example of the power of true love cannot be found.

UNITY

Theoretically, there are countless aspects in which we, ourselves, differ from other human beings: in religion, nationality, skin color, our interests, our opinions, our character traits, etc. Whenever we compare ourselves to another person, condemn someone and emphasize the difference between us and someone more than that which is connecting us, we create an inner and outer separation, by raising or lowering ourselves. We draw a frontier line, which makes a heart encounter impossible. Even worse, in unfavorable circumstances, fronts, parties, and positions can build up insurmountable walls, and in the worst case, they can cause violence or war.

Each time we condemn someone and emphasize the differences between ourselves and another human being, more than what unites us, we also create a separation and fragmentation in our own consciousness. We reject the fact that the shadow we project in others exists in our own consciousness. Only if we realize the «I in the You» and the «You in the I», we will be able to see what unites us and we will be inspired and enriched by diversity. At this point, true encounter can happen and we recognize that we are all ONE. In truth, there exists only ONE humanity, and only ONE religion: that of humanity and that of love.

A consciousness of unity does not mean that we all need to be or to become equal, but that the uniqueness of two people is no longer a problem. Living together with other beings is no longer based on convictions. We follow the motto «living and let living». We go with those people who are in resonance with our own soul frequency.

The consciousness of unity will be the consciousness of the coming age. For this reason, we are called to encounter our fellow humans more and more, from the perspective of unity. We can practice this by observing ourselves and by increasing awareness, where we are still creating separations. Then in a next step, we choose thoughts, words, and actions that create unity.

If we are able to recognize that we all have a common origin and that in all of us, the same divine essence rests, the world will find unity. Then the various forms of being and life can exist peacefully side by side. Tolerance arises when we accept the existing differences, when we focus on the essence of others and when we encounter each other authentically and lovingly, despite possible differences of opinion. Everyone can be and remain a friend in this way.

At this point could arise the question of how to deal with people who are full of negativity and whose influence is difficult to escape, like work colleagues or family members. There is not the one and only solution. It is important to look from situation to situation which response is appropriate. At this point, however, I would like to give two suggestions as inspiration.

On the one hand, we can try to distinguish between the ego and the soul of a person by making ourselves aware that this egoistic behavior is the expression of our separation from the divine source. If we keep this in mind, it is easier for us to take the other person's behavior less personally and to take a more compassionate attitude. In addition, we can try to focus primarily on the positive in the other human being, and to strengthen the good, by ignoring the destructive behavior and remaining open to them, by reacting calmly, authentically and lovingly.

As long as we take the behavior of the other person personally and something in us reacts emotionally, there is still something to correct in our own consciousness, from the perspective of the soul consciousness. If we feel hurt our ego consciousness was touched and we get the chance to learn something about ourselves.

Another way to behave in such a situation is to draw healthy boundaries when we are exposed to situations and energies that harm us, like violence or abuse. Boundaries can be a powerful «No» to manipulation, violence, negativity, and strong egoism. Through our «No» we signal that we do not accept and support destructive behavior. Moreover, they are a form of self-love that can help us to end dependencies and suffering. Especially for internal healing processes, sometimes it can be important that we temporarily retreat from a person or situation, or even remove ourselves completely from a relationship when there is strong egoism. This, too, is an option. However, even in these situations, we can also always be aware that the person carries a divine essence with which we are connected to. Taking this perspective creates unity on a higher level. It helps us to forgive and maybe to take a step forward together.

IN HARMONY WITH THE LAWS OF NATURE

Most people play a game that is called life and do not know the rules of the game. They do not know that there are spiritual laws of nature that affect the material world and their lives from the subtle spheres. These, for example, include the law of resonance, the law of love, the law of cause and effect, etc. Neither parents, nor school, nor university has taught us these laws. They are the key to happiness and fulfillment in life. Caring about them and living our lives according to them, takes us to joy, fullness, happiness, balance, and harmony. If we do not consider them, we create painful experiences and suffering.

Because many people do not know these laws, they often have to learn through suffering, and sometimes go through several lives of painful lessons. If one day they get the chance to hear about the laws, they begin to understand that they are the creators of their lives and that they have created what they experience in their lives.

When they begin to live according to these laws, then their lives change for the better, even sometimes surprisingly quickly.

To live in harmony with the laws of nature will be of great importance in Satya Yuga. It is recommended to deal more intensively with the topic.

BE HAPPY!

Many people think that they can´t be happy until certain circumstances or conditions have been fulfilled in their lives. The idea of happiness in many people is connected to beliefs and expectations: «Once I have 100,000 euros in my account, I am free and can travel.» or «If I am together with this woman or man I am happy.» or « If I have a child, then I will be happy.» or «If I have this job, in particular, everything will be fine.»

Often it happens that desired life circumstances sometimes do not occur in our lives or perhaps only as a temporary phenomenon. Therefore, if we make our happiness and joy of life dependent on external circumstances, we can fall into deep depression when the circumstances change or no longer fulfill our expectations.

Just as we are the source of unconditional love and inner peace, we are also the source of joy. No matter what kind of external circumstances surround us. We have the choice to decide whether we want to be happy or to suffer.

To be in a kind of lack-consciousness is a sure guarantor that we keep happiness away from us. In lack-consciousness, we have the feeling that something is missing in our happiness. We seek the satisfaction of our unfulfilled needs in the outside world. Through this, we become needy and beggars.

The paradox is that the universe will only increase our happiness and give us more abundance when we decide to see happiness in what we have. Then we live out of the consciousness of fulfillment. For this, it is important to uncover our inner lacks and to transform them, and to decide in every situation consciously: «TO BE HAPPY!»

GRATITUDE

Often we take for granted what is given to us by life. It is normal for us, especially in the western countries, that we get medical care, that warm water comes out of the tap, that we have a roof over our head that we can go to school, that we have enough to eat, and to grow up in peace.

If ever we were in a life situation, where we had to do without one or more of these aspects, we learn to be humble and grateful for what we have. Our living conditions could be quite different and could change at any time. Gratitude, also as unconditional love, produces the highest vibrational frequency.

It comes from the consciousness of fulfillment. If we express gratitude, we affirm that we acknowledge and accept the fullness of our life situation. As a result, life will give us more gifts.

Gratitude can be expressed immediately in the moments in which we feel it, by a short prayer or in the evening by reflecting on our day, and also by writing in a kind of diary or journal, about what we are thankful for in our lives.

SERENITY

Serenity is the ability to face all situations with a certain kind of relaxation, distance and equanimity, and not to be disturbed by the surrounding and immediate circumstances. With a calm attitude, we are anchored in basic trust and know that everything will fit in the right way at the right time.

Serenity does not mean to be indifferent. Indifference comes from the ego and is associated with disinterest and ignorance. In a state of indifference, there is generally no motivation to work for the improvement of a situation, or the well-being of other people and that of the earth. In a serene attitude, on the other hand, we are dedicated. Our actions are centered and we do not allow our mind to get carried away by thoughts and emotions. If we notice for example, that the things we try do not work out, we let go and look for new opportunities that are in harmony with our energy flow.

Serenity is an important part on the spiritual path. Through practice, we learn to distinguish when it is important to act and to engage, and when it is important to let go, to relax, to trust and, if necessary, to look for new possibilities. We are in a position to identify the right time and take advantage of the opportunities that arise.

FORGIVENESS

What are mistakes? To make mistakes is a part of the human evolution process and an important source of self-realization. Mistakes occur especially through ignorance of our true nature, and when we let ourselves be guided by our selfish motives. Mistakes are of great importance for our development process. They help us to develop distinctiveness in relation to what is working or not working in our lives, and what is useful or not useful for our development. By recognizing and transforming them, we have the opportunity to correct the path we have taken.

If we are afraid of making mistakes, we will always remain in a kind of comfort zone and we will limit the possibilities of our inner development. If we dare to engage in new experiences and allow ourselves to make mistakes in this context, we are expanding and growing. We get the chance to recognize the limitation of our thinking and behavioral patterns, to leave them and to elevate ourselves to a higher form of BEING. We allow ourselves to expand into our highest possibilities. This brings us more closely into our original nature.

Many people are afraid to make mistakes because they are consciously or unconsciously afraid to be condemned, punished, or rejected. Through this fear, they block their own process of growing. There are many people who do not react mildly, in proportion, or in a conciliatory and compassionate way to the mistakes of their fellow and separate themselves from others over the smallest thing. This makes it difficult on both sides to walk towards each other and to clarify and dissolve unpleasant situations through understanding and compassion.

It is the ego that is holding the old hurts and does not allow forgiving. It keeps the antagonism in people alive. If we are the ones who have made a mistake or the one who cannot forgive yet, from the perspective of nature we will be bound to a conflict until we have gone through the necessary development and have made the steps towards truthfulness, love, and forgiveness. Only then will we become free.

Forgiveness

If someone has hurt us, we should ask ourselves how we would wish to be treated if we would regret a mistake. We would all wish to be treated with gentleness, conciliation, and compassion, and to have the chance to correct our mistake.

Only if we cease to condemn other people because of their faults, if we even ignore their small mistakes and focus instead on their good being inside, then transformation, peace, and healing will happen for all of us and the earth too. This does not mean that we have to ignore our own emotions and processes. More it means to remove oneself from blaming and to take responsibility for one's own injuries and to engage in a healing process in the direction of forgiveness. Forgiveness is important for us to regain our inner freedom. It brings peace of soul back into one's own heart and of course, relieves the heart of someone else from any sense of guilt.

Everything can be forgiven, even if some processes of forgiveness are more challenging than others and take more time. There are strong stories of people who have forgiven happenings that many people would think impossible. At this point, I would like to recall the example of the man who had killed his former partner and her child. He transformed his own life through the unconditional love and forgiveness of the mother and grandmother of the murdered daughter and her child. They are ideal examples and can inspire anyone to be conciliatory, especially when it comes to seemingly banal things in everyday life.

Self-forgiveness

But it is not just about forgiving other people, but also forgiving ourselves. Often, people are merciless judges of themselves, and reject themselves for mistakes that have been made. Many people find it much easier to forgive others, then to forgive themselves. The «cannot forgive myself», keeps the mind fixed in the past, and in this way blocks its own developmental process.

It is important to accept that we are human beings and that as long as we have not fully returned to our divine original nature, we will make mistakes. If we succeed in seeing them as a gift and willingly accepting them, they will quickly lead us into greater self-knowledge and maturity and will enable us to make great progress. From a divine point of view, at every moment of our lives, we get a chance to change our lives.

How we can practice forgiveness

Forgiveness can be practiced in different ways. On the one hand, by encountering others without prejudice, and trying to understand them from their background and intentions. Everyone has a story to tell, from which his SO-BEING can be explained. When we look at this story, we get a holistic picture of the person. On closer inspection, facets become visible of the life of the other, which touch our compassion and which mitigate the condemnation and gravity in our reproaches.

Often, it is also the case that a person has an intention in a situation that is very different from what we perceive. Many people react prematurely to their own interpretation, without going into dialogue and striving to truly understand the depths behind. This creates a lot of separation in relationships. If we belong to those who judge quickly and give others no opportunity, we should reflect and consider whether or not we can take a step towards this person, to seek the dialogue, and at least try to get it from a greater depth of understanding.

If we are among those who do not get a chance to clarify, we must learn to accept the situation as it is and to come to peace with it, even if a pain remains.

If someone has made a mistake and we feel that we are hurt, we can be aware that we are the ones who decide whether to feel hurt or not. In this way, we can protect ourselves from destructive energies. If we have already allowed the energy to enter into us, we should strive directly in a process of forgiveness to come back to our inner peace.

To succeed in the process of forgiveness, it is important that we take care of our needs and feelings. Sometimes a spatial and temporal distance may be important and necessary to be able to see perspectives more clearly, to gain new insights and to heal and to release injured feelings.

We can also practice forgiveness by praying for people who have violated us. There is a prayer with which one can complete the day in a wonderful way, and to internally clean up unfavorable situations. It is said: «I forgive all those who have hurt me with or without intention. And I ask all those for forgiveness, which I have hurt with or without intention. I forgive and forgive myself. I send all light, love, and blessing, and I sincerely pray that only the best is done for everyone.»

Another way to strengthen our ability in forgiving is to think about how it can be possible to help the other person to reconnect with their good nature. Often the affected person suffers terribly from their own behavior and is desperate because, no way out of the behavioral pattern is visible. We can assume that a person who is choleric for example, is not happy with his reaction, even if he is not aware of this always. His choleric behavior separates him from others and leads him into solitude. At some point in his life, maybe he has suffered an injury that leads him to this kind of reaction. This injury needs compassion and not a rejection to be able to heal. In this context, compassion doesn't mean to endure all attacks as an affected person, but to take an inner attitude of compassion on a higher level, while at the same taking the steps that are necessary. It is not about nurturing dependencies, but about preserving one's own inner peace.

REPENTANCE

The ability to repent is of great importance on our spiritual path. Through repentance, we can stop, alter, and turn unfavorable creative processes that we have initiated, through ignorance or egoistic behavior into good ones. Repentance is the readiness to acknowledge a mistake and to correct the thinking and behaviors that have led to it, by replacing it with higher perspectives. At the moment of remorse, the thick walls of the ego get melted and are transformed by increased sensibility and humility.

The spiritual path is comparable to climbing a mountain. The top of the mountain symbolizes the divine perspective. It is the highest perspective a person can realize. The further we climb the mountain, the more we become an approach the highest point of view. On our way to the top, we encounter many obstacles: our patterns, illusions, mistakes, and habits. They are responsible for the fact that once we stepped down from the mountaintop.

Repentance is important in order to make progress on the spiritual path. It opens the door to higher cognition and to a superior perspective on ourselves and our lives. Through repentance, we throw old beliefs and life concepts, which are no longer useful to us, overboard and raise ourselves up to a higher level of consciousness. When we reach the point at which we have fully regained the divine perspective, we are in harmony with the creation. At this point, we live the highest version and the highest possibilities of our being.

I would like to share a story that I have heard during a meditation retreat. It is about a king who killed many people and caused much suffering for many families. In the course of his journey, he met Buddha. Buddha instructed him in a meditation technique. He began meditating and purified his consciousness from all selfish motives.

From a certain point in time, he felt much regret for what he had done. While meditating on his own, he had to feel the pain that he had inflicted on others. In spite of the cruel deeds he had committed, one day he attained the liberation of his soul.

After becoming enlightened, he went into the villages where he had taken the lives of children, husbands, and wives. When they recognized him, they threw stones at him, insulted him and spat at him. Without reacting, he let everything happen. In an attitude of great humility, he asked for forgiveness. When people realized that he had really changed and had become a source of love and peace, they forgave him. Thus, he initiated many people into Buddhist meditation and helped them move towards self-liberation.

The story shows that, no matter what we have done so far in our lives, we always get a new chance from nature when we truly deeply regret our former actions. Although the king's actions were cruel, by repentance he could attain the divine grace and still achieve the highest goal of life. Society may judge a man to the end of his life for his deeds. But from the point of view of nature, it is different. If we have balanced what we have created, we are free.

In a physical body, it is much easier for a person to be confronted with their deeds, to repent, to transform their own mistakes, and turn towards light, than in the worlds beyond. From the viewpoint of nature, it is very recommended that we use our time wisely on earth.

Spiritual Community

Many spiritual people have the feeling they are outsiders in Kali Yuga. They often feel as strangers in the material world and have the feeling of being forced into a system that does not correspond to their true nature. Because in Kali Yuga they are not in a majority, the likelihood of receiving encouragement and support from family and friends is not so high. Many of them are misunderstood for their high thoughts and ideas, by normal society and are sometimes confronted with criticisms. This is not easy, especially at the beginning of the spiritual path.

The wonderful thing is that the divine consciousness connects his awakening children to one another so that they are not alone in the spiritual way, and thereby we can become strengthened.

A spiritual community is a meeting place for like-minded people. It can exist in various forms. For example as a communal living together community, as group meetings, as satsang, or as prayer groups, etc. For the spiritual person, the community can be a kind of anchor. It can be a place where he can have an exchange and be given the necessary strength to face the challenges of the material world. For a spiritual person, who becomes energetically more and more sensitive, it is not always easy to find their place in the harsh everyday life of contemporary society and to maintain their energy level in a stable way. In the community, we can recharge, get inspiration, and feel that we are not wrong as we are. Moreover, it is the ego-based system that humanity itself has created, that is the cause of this. The spiritual human being has simply decided to uncover the untruths, and so to overcome the separation and ignorance of one's own true nature.

Many people are reluctant to walk on their own spiritual path because they fear exclusion and rejection. They fear either to be excluded by their families, partners, and friends, or, to be challenged by the spiritual path to a point where life could initiate changes that appear unknowable, and therefore fearful and dangerous. Almost everyone who decides in the Kali Yuga to walk the spiritual path is confronted with these fears at the beginning of his inner journey.

The spiritual path can be very challenging. It requires courage and strength to stand up for one's own truth. But when we reach the point where we fully say «YES» to the way that leads us to authenticity, we are then able to accept the challenges that come our way. We know that everything that happens, serves us only for our own good, to come closer to our true selves.

It is a part of the spiritual path that we learn more and more to trust that everything that belongs to us will come into our lives at a certain time and that everything that no longer belongs to us will go so that something better can arrive.

In the end, it will become apparent that those who have the courage to go their own way, despite all the skeptics, will lead a much happier and freer life. The truth will always win.

The spiritual community can encourage and strengthen us to stay on the path and to defy all opposition, and obstacles. The good news is that we are becoming greater in numbers, more and more people are on the way and in this way, it does become easier!

Living Your Own Soul Plan

Each soul is blessed with individual powers and fulfills an individual and unique role and task in the creation plan. Some souls, for example, are born to be leaders. Others are born to be artists, servants, healers, administrators, organizers, teachers or musicians, and so on. A human being can also carry several gifts at the same time, of course.

In Kali Yuga, many people play roles that do not correspond to their true natures. They superficially fulfill the expectations of others, mostly those of the family, the school, the profession, etc. A lot of times the primary motive behind actions is money and recognition.

In Kali Yuga it is not easy to find one's own soul path and to take one's own place in the universal plan of creation. The individual faces a society that largely ignores the divine essence. This is one reason why it requires a lot of strength and courage from the individual to oppose the predominant counter-forces of the Kali Yuga.

In Satya Yuga, it will be important that we find those tasks and roles that have been assigned to us by the Divine. Only they lead us to inner fulfillment and joy.

What most people do not know in this context is that their soul energy plays a key role according to the energetic balance of the Earth and that they serve the balance of the earth if they joyfully unfold their inner light.

LISTEN TO THE INNER VOICE

In Satya Yuga, people live completely in the soul consciousness. Their ways are guided mainly by their intuition. In this way, everyone is always in the right place at the right time and is brought together with the people with whom they should be together with, at a specific point in time. That is why it is important to prepare, to draw the attention inside and listen to the inner again.

We can clearly perceive the inner voice when the activity of the mind has been quietened. People who are very rational tend to have a harder time to hear the quiet intuitive voice. Their increased mental activity superimposes upon the intuition. Because in school, university and work, the rational ratio is the main focus that is developed and promoted; the majority of people continue to live and design their lives from the rational level and ignore their intuition.

When we ignore the inner voice, we often have to learn our lessons through suffering. But even these kinds of experiences are important. They lead us to greater realizations.

For people who are naturally attached to their souls, the inner voice is their inner compass, guiding them from their heart. They can recognize the signs sent to them by the divine consciousness. They interpret them in the right way and act according to them. This is the key to open up the door to miracles in life. For the rational man, the actions of the soul do not always seem logical and comprehensible. However, people who allow the guidance of their soul to act upon them understand each other. They speak the same language.

There are some criteria by which we can orientate ourselves and recognize whether we experience an intuition or is it an impulse from the ego? Information that comes from the soul has a supernatural character. It impresses with a feeling of clear knowledge that cannot always be explained rationally. We know, without knowing from where. This inner truth is immovable and withstands every testing. Even if we want to ward it off or do not want to admit it, we are always led to the point where we have to acknowledge the truth.

If we touch moments that are related to the intuitive voice, we seem to flow effortlessly into events. It feels like the way is already open for us and we just have to go on it.

In this way, there are feelings of joy, lightness, serenity, and peace. Sometimes a cleansing pain can be felt. This happens when we are asked to let go of old life patterns and concepts, for higher ones. If we follow our intuitions, they immediately bring good fruits to us.

However, when we follow the impulses from the ego, we experience how the flow of life gets stuck. We immediately suffer energy losses and feel entangled and weighed down. We may also feel that we are being held back and/or treading on the spot. The meaning behind this experience is that we are invited from within, to look more closely and to realize at which point we have not acted in harmony, with our soul and the laws of nature. One could understand this process as a loving educational measure by nature. Emotions that belong to the ego are jealousy, envy, anger, fear, shame, guilt, excitement, etc. If we follow these impulses, they burden us and our interpersonal relationships. Once we have learned our lessons and corrected our behavior, our life will flow more smoothly again.

How quickly we learn our lessons, depends on ourselves. We can learn them within a few seconds or within several lives. The best is to try to learn them right away. In this way, we spare ourselves and those around us, a lot of needless suffering and time, and we can enjoy the higher possibilities of the soul more quickly. Mostly we can find our own mistakes by asking ourselves, where did I not act in unconditional love?

An individual relationship to the Divine

For the upcoming world change, a personal relationship to the divine will be of great importance. It will give us the necessary protection in the forthcoming time.

In Satya Yuga, we will be connected naturally to the Divine in our hearts again. It doesn't matter if we belong to a religion or not. Nor does it matter in whose name we worship the Divine. This may be the divine aspect with which we feel more connected, such as Jesus, God, Babaji, Buddha, Krishna, Shiva, Mary, Hunab'Ku, Wakan Tanka, Aloah, Allah, etc. If we have a problem with all these divine names, we can also choose a name that is in harmony with us, such as All-encompassing Consciousness, Great Power, Creator or Divine Nature. The name chosen is not all-important. That we are, and how we are, in a personal relationship with the Divine is what is important. Here only essential qualities count, like unconditional trust, love, peace, forgiveness, freedom, devotion, and faith.

Again and again, I encounter people who have experienced in their childhood that fanatical teachers, or their grandparents or parents, have tried to impose the faith of the Christian church or other faiths traditions on them, by force. They have experienced emotional and physical abuse in this context. To this day, we can see how, in the name of God, parts of the world are fighting each other. This restrictive and unfree created image of

God, which shows itself to many people viewing it who are uninvolved, of course, creates resistance in a very understandable way.

Yet this image has been created exclusively by man himself and has nothing to do with spirituality, and the divine consciousness itself. From a human point of view, it's about dogmatism, power, ignorance, and selfishness. The divine, on the other hand, is universality, peace, supreme love and freedom!

The problem of many people is that their resistance to these unwanted outside pressures, then also block the unique connection to the Divine in their hearts. I encourage everyone to become aware of their injuries and projections, to dissolve them, and to approach the divine in the heart in a new, unbiased and free way. The encounter with God is intimate, personal and individual.

For this, we don't have to join any religion or spiritual direction. However, if one is especially attached to a tradition, one can connect to that path that corresponds to one's own being. I have read a wonderful saying from a Sufi master, which still accompanies me, and touches me still today. The meaning of the saying is that a truly spiritual person can encounter God equally in the church, in a mosque, in a synagogue, in nature, in a Hindu temple, or in a sweat lodge. God is in us all time and lives in our hearts. God is the dark and the light at the same time, but in his essence, he is unconditional love, is harmony and peace, is creativity and joy that radiates out of itself. He is the spark of divinity in us, which is an image of his glory, to which we can flourish with too, if we purify the consciousness of selfishness. The dark was only created that we are able to see his light in us, beyond the game of duality. To experience His glory is what He truly wants us to experience, through our soul.

I would like to share a poem that I wrote in September 2015. I myself had to go through a process in which I had to dissolve many projections in my relationship to the divine. This poem crowned the conclusion of my own healing process. At this point, I would like to publish it with the intention and hope that it can serve and inspire other people who may be in their own process.

A POEM

GOD - WHO ARE YOU?

I am the most loving feeling in your heart,
Which you always long for,
If you have only experienced it once!
I am your loveliest action,
Your loveliest word,
Your most loving thought,
To bring joy to you, and others!
I am the one, who is always there and never leaves you,
Not even,
When you get entangled in the confusions of your life
And you take other things more importantly than me.

I am the one, who never imposes more than you can
carry,
Who is full of confidence and faith in you,
That you can do everything that I have asked you for
And that you are even bigger afterwards.

I am the one who always loves you.
I am the one, who blesses you, protects you,
Who turns everything into good,
If you give me your life,
Love me
And trust me and put me first in everything.
I am the one who gives you everything.

I am the one who looks at you with love and
understanding.
I am the one who is there when you call and ask Him with
All of your heart
And move the whole universe and hoists all the flags,
To give you the answer.
The one who uses all creation and sets signs,
So that you can hear it.
I am the one who can never be called fruitless.

I am the one who is always stable,
I am your home, where your origin is.
I am the one who is only one thought far away from you,
when you leave your home.
I am the one who will never turn away from you,

No matter how many issues and doubts you have.
I am your father and your mother at the same time.
Strong and determined, gentle and soft!
You are my children, all equally loved,
I am the one who never withdraws his love.

I am the one who knows all his children
And who gives you everything,
When you are ready to receive.
I am the infinite fullness, the healing, and the light.
I am the one, who holds and fulfills what he promises
if you trust my words.
I am the one who only gives two rules for happiness:
To love me and others.
I am only here to give, to give, to give.

I am the one who waits
That you come back to me from the material creation,
To run towards my arms again,
That you can experience the highest light and happiness,
The highest joy and love.

I am the one who always sends you opportunities,
and never stop it
until you are back in my arms.
My love always remains a voluntary offer to you.

I'm the one who already forgave you,
Before you forgive yourself,

and who teaches you to forgive yourself and others.

I am the one who gives you a place for your uniqueness,
Who nourishes your soul and refreshes your heart with
ecstasy and joy.
Who sends you nourished out into the world.
You are my unique creature.

I am the infinite knowledge, the truthfulness,
The one with the thousand names that always knows
Which is the best for you.

I am the one who works through you and
Guides you quietly
And brings you to your greatest thought
and actions,
But never insists.

I am the one who knows you
to the last corner of your being.

I am the one, who is always joyful and loving,
Blessing and accepting.
I am the one who lets you know if you experience and
know him:
That you yourself are the creator.

POEM FROM
STEPHANIE BUNK, SEPTEMBER 2015

Some people ask me in lectures if God is love, then how he can allow such great suffering in the form of wars and natural disasters. They say that this would only strengthen the image of a punitive God. Then I answer them that it is we, the human beings ourselves, who have created the current situation, by ignoring the laws of nature and by using our free will with ego. It has very little to do with the divine source itself. By our free will, we have decided to wage wars and misuse the Earth as we currently do. Our soul has also voluntarily decided to get involved in the earthly experience with all its current realities. In addition, we are constantly given opportunities, warnings, and help from the divine, to change our situation.

But the problem is that many people are so caught in their ignorance, that they are unaware of the urgency of changing the current situation, or of even taking it seriously. As a result, we overlook the opportunities that are offered to us. What happens currently is an act of love and not a punishment. The earth and the people get the chance to heal. But without our cooperation, it is not possible.

WAYS TO THE DIVINE

Many spiritual masters provide us with important clues on how we can build our relationship with the Divine and gain His grace in this age of Kali Yuga. The most important aspects are karma yoga, prayer, and the continual repetition of one of the many names of God.

Karma Yoga

In the age of Kali Yuga, «karma yoga» is one of the highest and most important forms of yoga. Karma Yoga is the selfless service for the good of humanity, the earth, and creation. Karma yoga includes all actions that improve the life and development of others, and of the Earth, in a constructive and positive way, in harmony with the laws of nature. Our actions for the good are offered to the divine without expecting and being attached to any particular result.

Any action can be karma Yoga. Our motives and intentions behind our actions decide if it is karma yoga or not. If our intention is materialistic and egoistically orientated, our action is not karma yoga. If it is performed selflessly, with devotion and love for God and with no view that the outcome Must go a certain way, then it is karma yoga. An example should make it clearer:

Today in the music industry, singers let music producers write their lyrics and make the musical arrangement of their songs. They want to become famous fast and to get far in the charts. They also want to earn a lot of money. Their basic motivation is material and egoistically orientated. This is not karma yoga.

A musician writes spiritual songs. He receives his texts in inspired moments. He also produces the music for the lyrics by himself. The whole process until the release of the CD is a creative act. He puts his whole heart and his love into his work.

He does his best at all levels. His intention is not to become famous and make a lot of money, but to worship God through his music and to touch the hearts of others. It is left to the divine if he will be successful with his music or not. For him, the process counts, and not what comes out of it in the end. The basic motivation of his action is selflessly serving. This is Karma Yoga.

The karma yogi generally does not favor any particular form of work. He considers every job as important and equivalent. No matter if it's about cleaning a toilet or making big talks. He works where he is needed and where he can use his skills to improve the life of others. The main motive of his work is to love and serve God. Therefore he sees an opportunity to serve God in any situation. By doing so, he gives consolation to those in need, helps where help is needed, etc.

A karma yogi also doesn't expect recognition and/or anything in return, for what he does for others. His giving is generous and unconditional. In deep trust in God, he knows that God knows his needs and that his needs get fulfilled by the divine source when he really needs something. Therefore, he always remains calm and prudent.

By practicing Karma Yoga, every person gets the opportunity to discover and develop their own abilities and their own inherent potential. He uses the developed gifts and abilities to serve the good of all. As a result, he grows beyond his limitations and expands his perspective on life.

Karma Yoga cleanses the heart and polishes the character of a human like a rough diamond being polished. A person who starts with karma yoga often first encounters many limitations and egoistic motives and gets the chance to transform them through selfless service. He gets gradually purified of his selfish motives, unfolds his inherent divinity and comes closer to his original divine essence.

Karma Yoga is the highest form of work a person can perform. Through karma yoga, we can gain the grace of God and dissolve our negative karma. This leads the soul to liberation from the wheel of rebirths. When the Divine blesses us with the opportunity to serve, we are invited to say wholeheartedly «Yes» and to perform the work with joy. We cannot imagine how big and important the blessing that follows will be for us.

PRAYER

Interestingly, prayers are an important part of all religious and spiritual traditions worldwide. Prayers have a great power. They can influence and change possible events in creation positively. Prayers are the greatest gift of all that we can give to another person and the Earth. Knowing this is of great importance, especially in the current turbulent times, because we have the opportunity to pray for the protection of other people and for as little suffering to happen as possible. Salvation lies in the spiritual world.

There exist interesting studies of the American professor Dr. William Brauds, and of the Japanese scientist, Masaru Emoto, that examined scientifically the influence of mental powers and prayers on subjects.

In a study, Dr. William Brauds was able to prove that the dying process of red blood cells could be prolonged if a group of 30 persons tried mentally to counteract their decay. The Japanese scientist Masaru Emoto could show that certain word vibrations, like love and hate, prayers and sounds affect the crystalline structure of water. Depending on the influence whether it is positive or negative, the crystalline geometric structure of water becomes harmonious or disharmonious.

Through prayers, we build and strengthen our relationship to the Divine. The highest form of prayer is the one that truly comes from the heart and happens in sincere love and devotion. This type of prayer directly reaches the divine, and it will promptly respond to this.

Depending on the situation, we can choose a form of prayer that is suitable for our current situation, like a prayer of gratitude, or a prayer for protection. We can also simply tell the divine source what moves our heart. During a prayer, we can talk to the Divine, as to a friend, a lover, a parent, or as a teacher.

In times of prayer, we are particularly receptive to the presence and guidance of the Divine. It can occur as a gentle, loving, groundbreaking feeling in our hearts or in the form of a depressing feeling, if it wants to point out our mistakes and will show us the need for correction.

Even though you may have been one of those people who did not believe in the existence of a higher power until now, you can simply start praying. You have nothing to lose, quite the opposite.

THE POWER OF THE NAME OF GOD

The Divine has innumerable names: God, Allah, Supreme Divine Consciousness, Higher Self, Hunab'Ku, Wakan Tanka, Aloah, Buddha, Krishna, Shiva, just to name a few. The name of God generates the highest harmonic vibrational energy frequency in the consciousness of man and in nature. It purifies the consciousness of attachments and selfishness, and so creates harmony, purity, love, peace, and joy.

When we consciously sing or chant the name of God, we connect ourselves with these positive essential qualities and invite them to work in our lives.

We can repeat the name of the divine for example, in the form of a mantra. Mantras play an important role in many spiritual and religious cultures. Through countless repetitions of masters and humans over the millennia, strong energetic fields have built up on the subtle level, into which we can engage through mantra recitation. Mantras work like the frequency controller of a radio. If you have set the right frequency, you can connect to the desired energy frequency.

Anyone can choose which form of mantra recitation suits to them and their path. In Sanskrit, there are for example the powerful mantras «Om Namah Shivaya« («Lord Thy will be done») or «Hare Krishna».

There is also the possibility of being given a mantra initiation by a master and receiving a personal mantra to practice with. That is the most charged one with divine light. It speeds up the inner development.

Following the Heart

Modern man is strongly driven by his material desires and wishes, like success, money, etc. He chases after his goals in the outer world and defines himself through their fulfillment. He suffers when the unexpected happens in his life that interferes with his plans. As a result, he is often confronted with tension, anxiety, restlessness and inner fights.

As long as he seeks in the outside world what he can only find in the interior, he will always be led to the point where he has to recognize that the pursuit of external wishes only leads to short-term joy and finally into nothing substantial. Depending on which karmic seeds a human carries within, some people recognize this earlier, others later.

At some point, tired of the experience of the emptiness of the material world, man begins to feel a yearning for something greater and embarks on a search for it. This moment marks a turning point in life and the beginning of the spiritual awakening.

From this point onwards, many people start to follow the spiritual path. They read books about spiritual subjects, seek inspiration from spiritual teachers, or visit events and seminars, etc. This time is an important phase that leads us to the point where we will find our spiritual home and our true individual roles and the tasks of our souls. Our spiritual path becomes more individual, focused, deeper and more purposeful. For example, we have arrived in a spiritual tradition with which we feel deeply connected, and that corresponds to our soul´s feeling. Or we have found a practice that deepens our inner path.

In this way, the self-will of man moves more and more into the background and divine guidance takes over our lives. Self-will in this context means ego-led will, which is based on self-centeredness. Man believes that only he is the one who can take care of the satisfaction of his needs. Sometimes people call a person self-willed when they are following their heart and do not fit into the social norm. Here a distinction is important. The ego-led will lead us away from God. On the contrary, if we follow our heart, which represents our soul's desire, we come closer to God.

Giving up the egoistic self-will is probably one of the most challenging steps on the spiritual path, but it is also the most beautiful. Man gives up the control of the ego and goes into his true serving spiritual identity. At that time, he has recognized deeply that his own egoistic wishes separate him from unity, and that he is ignorant and limited in access to the light and wisdom of God. He confidently gives his life into God's hands and completely entrusts himself to His wisdom and knowledge.

At this point, many people are scared that they might lose their identity. However, this is not the case and only a fear of the ego.

At this point, we simply give up our false identity, which is based on false reaction patterns and beliefs. We elevate ourselves to a higher level of BEING. This BEING is much more joyful, fulfilled, loving and lovely than the ego ever could be.

To take this step, it is important that we first strengthen our trust in God by becoming aware that his nature is completely good, and filled with unconditional love for us. His will wishes the best for everyone and wants to lead us to the highest harmony, fulfillment, and joy.

Having experienced a few times how miracles unfold if we trust God completely, one knows about that power and love. We also know that no one in the world will ever be able to give us what the divine is able to give us. Because it knows us like no other human and it knows us more than we do ourselves. It knows about our true identity and wants to lead us to this. The divine knows our strengths, tasks, and weaknesses with which we have incarnated on earth. It also knows about our true needs and wishes to fulfill them on all levels.

Living in harmony with our true identity, life becomes mature, free, loving, peaceful, joyful, harmonious, deep and fulfilled.

When we feel that we have entangled ourselves in the desires of our ego, we can pray to God and say: «Please lead me to my truth», or «Father, you know what I really need. I trust you» or «Bring my life in harmony with your will and let me live my highest being». Then we free ourselves from our low egoistic desires and open the door for all the things that correspond to our true spiritual desires. We invite them to come into our lives. However, we must accept that the Divine fulfills them in his own way and often not as we expect.

RESPECT CREATION

The earth gives us all we need to live with great selflessness. She gives us the land that we can cultivate and inhabit so that we have a home. It gives us tasty food, air to breathe, water to drink, herbs to heal. Everything that exists on earth was originally pure and was made in love for humanity, to serve its well-being, joy, and salvation. But through increasing egoism and greed, man has destroyed the purity of the earth and made himself and nature sick. Humans, animals, plants and the earth are connected via a unifying universal field of consciousness. Nothing exists independently. Everything that happens within this field of consciousness is in interaction with each other. If we as the human species behave destructively towards nature, it has destructive effects on all other living beings too. However, if we are loving and mindful towards creation and other living beings, we strengthen the healing powers.

To respect the creation means to treat all living beings equally with care, love, and respect. This includes the plant and animal world, our fellows, and Mother Earth. If all humans would live in that consistently, there would be no more wars and we would create a paradise on earth.

How can we help nature return to its original purity and how can we come out from the one-sided relationship with the Earth? How can we bring paradise back to Earth? There are many ways we can work for a better world, even on a smaller scale. Every little positive action is significant. At this point, a few topics will be touched upon and can serve as an inspiration.

BUILDING UP POWER PLACES

Building power places is important because they strengthen the Earth's energetic balance. A power place is a place with a particularly high vibration, which radiates into the environment. When you stay at this place, your own vibration is raised and you feel more powerful, peaceful, harmonious and joyful. It is also easier to connect with higher states of consciousness.

We can make a contribution to positive change in the world by creating power places in our homes, and by inviting the spiritual world to work through it. Creating a power place is actually very easy.

First, one selects lovingly a suitable place in one's living space, or in the garden. There you can build an altar. You can set up a small table, place a tablecloth on it and then put personal items on it, such as images of a spiritual teacher, candles, crystals, aroma lamp, etc. Creativity has no bounds.

Energetically, we can strengthen the energy of the place, amongst other things, by meditating, lighting incense sticks and candles daily, offering food to the spiritual world, as well as praying and practicing small rituals. There are Vedic ceremonies like the «Arati» (light-ceremony) or «Agni Hotra» (fire ceremony) as examples, which purify the atmosphere and increase the light of the place. The ritual doesn't necessarily have to be of Vedic origin. It can spring from the tradition one feels most connected to. Most importantly is that it is done with an attitude of love and with heart.

I would like to share a personal experience that has touched me deeply: When I opened the Yoga- and Siddhazentrum in Markdorf in May 2014, it was important for me to find a daily ritual for my spiritual teachers Agastya Rishi and Lubamitra, to be able to express my love for them. I learned the Arati during my yoga teacher training and so I started practicing it daily in the morning and in the evening. An arati is a ceremony in which light is offered in front of an altar and connects to the spiritual world while reciting certain mantras.

In the beginning, I was still uncertain in my worship ceremony. I lit incense sticks and candles every day, as I had learned in the Indian temples. Sometimes I put fruit on the altar, sometimes I didn´t.

One day I received a message from Agastya and Lubamitra through the Jiva Nadi. They told me that they are very happy with the Arati and the lights I light daily in the center. But sometimes I would offer fruits and sometimes not. I should always offer fruits to them.

The message touched me deeply. Since then, there are always fruit or sweets in the center, which I distribute to the students. Through the Arati, the fruit becomes Prasadam. Prasadam is blessed food.

SELF-SUFFICIENCY

Last summer, I passed three cherry trees on a walk that was full of red cherries. The bright red cherries just smiled at me and I had to taste them. They were unbelievably tasty and sweet. Two weeks later I returned to the same place. The cherries hung rotten and unpicked on the tree.

In the last years, I often perceived this kind of situation. It is always unbelievable to me that a society can afford it to leave healthy and energetically life-giving fruits hanging on the tree. And furthermore prefer instead food that is denatured, energy deficient, pathogenic, and with pesticide residues from a supermarket.

In my opinion, this reflects the relationship of the current human being to nature. The current situation with regard to food should make us very thoughtful and is terrifying. It makes clear how great the separation of man from nature has become now. It used to be natural to live in harmony with nature and to cultivate organic food. Nowadays, the seeds are genetically modified. Humans need organic labels to mark the purity of the food. And even then it is not guaranteed that the labels are really trustable. In addition to that, a large part of the harvest is simply thrown away because it does not fit with the legal guidelines in terms of shape.

In the age of media, man's natural instincts seem to be dulled and the intuitive impulses from the inside are overlaid with artificial ones. Many people appear gray, oversaturated, unhappy, and lifeless. The rise of psychiatric illnesses in civilization speaks for itself. Out of the material abundance, we are barely able to appreciate the gifts of nature.

It is time that we change our behaviors towards nature. If many people are willing to reshape their living areas according to their possibilities, to bring harmony back to nature, we can make a huge change together. We should not wait until movements are initiated by politicians. It is a change that the people themselves should initiate. The time is running. Many politicians seem to want to ignore the explosive force of the situation. Instead of focusing on this issue, capitalism and the preservation of power positions are still given priority.

There are some good initiatives that you can join to engage in these developments. One initiative, for example, is: «Earth in balance». It was founded in May 2017. You will find further information under:

www.earth-in-balance.org.

We should always remember that Mother Earth, like humans and animals too, is a living being. She suffers when wars are waged on her body and people are full of selfishness, negativity, and hatred. She is happy when people dedicate themselves to her with love and care. And just as love and care bring healing to humanity; it also brings it to the earth.

What can we do to return to a natural life? First of all, as already indicated, it is of great importance to create habitats in which nature can recover from its artificial treatment and return to its original natural cycles. We can make a big contribution to change if we, for example, use our gardens or balconies for self-sufficiency and reshape them in a way that nature's cycles can recover and naturally unfold. For this, we should only use methods that are in harmony with nature, like «permaculture» (permanent agriculture) or biodynamic agriculture. Above all, it is important to make sure, without compromise, not to use genetically modified seeds and conventional fertilizers.

There exist great ideas about how unused areas in cities can be managed organically. For example, there are projects in which beds are created on unused land, where people of different ages and cultures come together, and cultivate the land.

It is also a great idea to join together with neighbors of the residential street and to think about how to transform the residential street in a collective and ecological way, so that part of our food needs can be produced on a self-sufficient basis together. The organization could be for example, in such a way that each garden, depending on space and solar radiation, grows certain crops, fruits, and vegetables that will later be shared with the neighborhood. If the street has many asphalted surfaces, raised beds could be built upon these. It would also be interesting to host bee colonies that supply the residential streets with honey all year round. Even chickens and cows that supply the inhabitants of a street with eggs and milk are possible.

The small projects together have the power to bring a lot of change in the world, if they arise in many places at the same time. In this context, we should also try to avoid food from companies that do not take social and environmental responsibility in production. Because when we support such companies we support the exploitation of the Earth. It is important to collect information about this issue and to make a choice.

Some large companies are now seeking to patent even seeds and to impose penalties on allotment gardeners, if their second generation seeds are detected in their gardens. In addition, they even secure seats in politics to influence the political decision-making in their favor. What the earth gives: water, land, seeds, air belongs to all people equally who live on earth and must be distributed fairly.

VEGETARIAN/ VEGANISM

If we want to get back in harmony with nature, it is also an important and necessary step that we become vegetarian or vegan. The high consumption of meat and milk by humans contributes to the imbalances on earth in a dramatic way.

Every day, millions of animals are slaughtered who previously had to live a cruel existence, just to serve people's wealth and insatiable greed. In conventional livestock farming, animals are penned up in the narrowest of spaces. Their everyday lives are characterized by violence and unkindness.

According to the Meat Atlas, in 2014 750,000,000 animals were slaughtered only in Germany, and worldwide it was around 150,000,000,000. The trend is still in an upward direction. For 1 kg of beef, 15,000 liters of drinking water is needed. 70 percent of the world's grain is grown to feed animals. To be able to feed all these animals, fields are over-exploited and over-fertilized.

Furthermore, according to the United Nations' Food and Agriculture Organization (FAO) report (Global Forest Resources Assessment, FRA 2010), 160,000 km² of rainforest was cut down, each year, between 1990 and 2000. In the years 2000 - 2010 there were 130,000 km ² cut down annually. Seventy percent of the land was used to create grazing land for animals and arable land for soya as animal feed. By comparison, Germany has a total territorial area of 357,000 km². Meanwhile, the deforestation rate is falling. But what damage is already caused by this? If you look at these facts, you can only shake your head. What a crime to nature! What a deep disrespect and ignorance of creation!

Many people ignore the hazards for health that are associated with the consumption of meat and milk from conventional livestock. They don´t realize that everything that has been done to the animal they also take into their body by eating meat. And that's a lot. First of all, the animals are fed with genetically modified soybean plants. They are injected with growth hormones so that they are able to grow faster and fatter. The animals are given prophylactic high doses of antibiotics because factory farming is a source of many pathogens. At slaughter, the animals release the stress hormone adrenalin into their flesh. Nobody knows if the piece of meat lying in front of him comes from an animal with a short or long-term death struggle, and can´t determine the actual level of adrenalin in the meat.

If the meat is processed after slaughter, it is preserved with nitrates and pickling salts to slow down the decomposition process. In addition, dyes are added to make the meat look fresher. After all this processing, the piece of meat ends up on our plate. Actually, it is nothing more than a piece of poison that is poisoning us. It has now been scientifically proven that meat consumption is a contributing factor to many diseases of civilization, such as cardiovascular diseases and cancer. Meat also makes the blood acid and disturbs the alkaline-based balance of the body.

From a yogic point of view, one looks even further and includes the energetic effects of meat consumption. According to yogic diet, meat is tamasic. Its consumption blocks the subtle energies and promotes an attitude of mind that is characterized by negativity and depressiveness. From an energetic point of view, we also nourish our inherent animalistic nature and lower-vibrating states of consciousness. In summary, this means that by consuming meat we burden our energy system and pollute it. This is independent of whether we consume meat from conventional or environmentally dynamic agriculture.

Whether we believe it or not, meat consumption and the way the animal lived have an impact on our physical, mental and spiritual balance. It is known in psychology that emotions are stored energetically in the cells of the body. This also applies to animals. The information about the kind of life experiences an animal had is stored in his cells. Through the consumption of meat, we absorb those cells into our own body, and thus also the stored information and emotions.

Meat consumption is completely unnecessary in our society today to survive. There are plenty of good food alternatives. The world hunger crisis would be solved if we were largely vegetarian or vegan and if we would use the arable land to grow crops to feed people. Then there would be enough food for all. After all, how can one world use most of the arable land to nourish animals that serve as secondary food, while a billion people starve? This is incomprehensible and is based on a sick system. Incidentally, the advantage of cereals is that they last much longer than meat and can be stocked for a longer period of time.

NEW SCHOOLS AND NEW EDUCATION CONCEPTS

Every child has an inborn curiosity and a natural scientific drive to discover the world on its own. It has a natural joy of learning and to ask questions about life. It seeks answers that help it to understand the world and what happens around it.

For many children, the joy of learning is already dampened shortly after starting school. Later the motivation gets even lower and in many cases completely lost. The natural joy of learning turns into learning frustration. How will a child be able to develop itself freely in an environment of pressure, evaluation, and anxiety? It becomes either an adapted «yes-man» or a rebel.

Schooling is a hard time for many children and families. Considering that a child goes many years of his life to school and is not really happy at that time, is terrifying. The school system, as it is now, has a great potential to frustrate all parties by suggesting to parents, teachers, and children that they are not good enough. The amazing thing is that everybody participates anyway. Because currently there are less good alternative schools, many parents and children still have to clench their teeth, to persevere and to survive the school time, somehow. Why do we not create schools where children feel happy and teachers can joyfully fulfill their inner vocation as a teacher? Why do we not initiate schools in which students, teachers, and parents spend beautiful and meaningful years together?

Once I did an internship in a clinic. There were special therapy groups for teachers. Several times I was allowed to participate in the group sessions and got deeper insights into the problems of being a teacher today. There were engaged teachers who had fallen into a burn-out. They were no longer capable to take the pressure that has increased in the last years upon them. There is a curriculum that is crammed with more and more knowledge contents and that feeds the children only rationally. Teachers are confronted with overcrowded classrooms and a growing number of children who come from unstable families and need special attention.

Teachers have become part of a system in which they are no longer able to follow their vocation with joy. There is more and more required of them and it is difficult to keep a healthy balance.

Studies have shown how important the relationship between teachers and students is for a good education for children. The more intense and better the relationship between teacher and student, the more the children learn. In the current school system, it seems to be overlooked that it is almost impossible for a single teacher, depending on the class and school type, to be able to provide a good relationship simultaneously, to 28-32 children in a class. It is clear that in such a system many children but also teachers perish. I am aware that there are exceptions. But the picture has not changed much over the last decade.

Now, it brings up the question of how can we change the school system in such a way that it produces free and happy people? Children who do not lose their joy of learning and who remember a happy school time? Children who are allowed to follow their own learning rhythm? Teachers who can follow their determination in an environment that respects a healthy balance? The answer is clear: it needs courageous teachers and people who see through all this madness, and are brave enough to build new schools that involve the wholeness of everybody. A healthy school system includes the holistic development of body, mind, and soul. It also cares about spirituality as well as community building and creativity. In addition, a school should know about the higher mental abilities of a person and should promote it.

An interesting school concept was set up in Tekos, Russia, by the Russian music teacher Michail Petrowitch Schetinin. The school was given a UNESCO award in 1998, as the best school in the world. The children themselves set the pace at which they work on topics and help each other in their learning processes. This prevents competitive situations. If the children are particularly interested in a subject, they can go on, in one subject, through the knowledge of eleven school classes within a year. If they have finished their classes, they can even visit the university on this subject. Every child is accompanied by a mentor or group of students that have the same or a higher level of the child's knowledge. Under the terms «LAIS» and «natural learning» can be found more information, on the internet.

An interesting school concept is also that of the democratic school. According to this concept, children can create their own learning processes, self-determined, in harmony with their learning rhythms. A wonderful film about this topic is called «Schools of trust».

Maybe you feel called and inspired to get involved in the field of new forms of education and to build new schools. If you want to be informed and look for inspiration, you can follow the link recommendations below.

Integrative Medical System

One tragedy that is currently happening in the medical system is that the medical sector seems to have degenerated into a corrupt system, dominated by the machinery of the pharmaceutical industry.

In this context, doctors and pharmacies are demonstrably bribed, studies are falsified and guidelines are changed arbitrarily, to achieve higher sales volumes for certain medical products.

There are also efforts to displace naturopathy and abolish other health professions, to fully control the drug market. One gets the impression that the current medical system is primarily orientated on profits and not on the healing of people.

Furthermore, the current medical system is characterized by many other imbalances. For decades, the personnel situation in many hospitals and nursing homes is one of chronic understaffing. The imbalances that are caused by this situation must be compensated by doctors and nurses, through an ever-increasing workload and work hours. Many health professionals are suffering more and more burn-outs. Almost everyone knows the situation of stressed doctors and nurses who do not really have time to treat the patient as a whole human being. In many hospitals, this creates an impersonal and disharmonious atmosphere that opposes the full recovery of many patients, and attacks the work-life balance of doctors and nursing staff.

It raises the question: How can a medical system that is not healthy in itself really cure ill people?

From an ayurvedic point of view, the nutrition of the patients in hospitals is more than catastrophic, in terms of the healing process. How can it be for example, that weakened people in hospital get cheap industrially produced food that is rajasic and tamasic, and is a burden to the body, and disturbing it's healing processes?

Especially if the patient is in a weakened situation, he needs freshly prepared food that gives him life energy and supports his healing process. I am convinced that if there would be openness to that issue, there would be ways and concepts that could make it possible, to realize healthy food in hospitals economically.

It seems to me that it is more important than ever that the patient remains self-responsible for his recovery process and doesn't hand it over completely at the doctor's door, or to the hospital. The patient should stay awake, should seek doctors who do not want to dominate him with an attitude of know-it-all better, but who cooperate also with him or her, in accordance with one's needs and desires. It needs a healthy mix of heart and mind. It is also crucial that we learn again to listen to the intuitive voice and to trust it. In this way, our intuition can lead us to the right helpers and will help us in our healing processes.

In my opinion, the medical sector needs major shifts in thinking on all levels, also in the image of man. In the conventional medical system, the world view still prevails that man is a mechanical and material being. This is also the guiding principle when it comes to develop treatment methods and medicines for different clinical situations. Pharmaceutical drugs largely affect human chemistry, without embracing man in his holistically psychic and spiritual dimensions. More and more people are turning to alternative healing methods for this reason. Because, in the contemporary medical system, they often do not find the kind of help and treatment they wish and want.

From the point of view of humanness, it is requisite that the medical system changes in such a way that it works completely benevolently for the patient. There should be a cooperation and synthesis between conventional and alternative health professions. Only then is it ensured that the patient is seen in their holistic way and that they are provided with an offer of the best treatment methods, from which they can choose for themselves, their own healing path in harmony with themselves and their convictions.

Instead of competing, there should be a cooperative atmosphere between the treating physicians, therapists, and other health professionals. There, in my opinion, is the biggest potential. For example, the conventional medical system is amazing in the field of surgery and emergency medicine. Alternative medical systems, which consider a human holistically and beyond its material aspects, are Ayurveda and TCM, as two examples.

Unfortunately, many doctors still have an ignorant and sometimes arrogant attitude toward alternative health care professions. Sometimes one gets the impression that they have appointed themselves as all-knowing authorities.

A synthesis of the various medical directions means an encounter at eye level between the respective professional groups and to acknowledge and appreciate the knowledge or non-knowledge of the other. It means to fertilize each other in a development process and to grow together. Then the treating team can make good decisions in the interests of the patient. This way has already been practiced in Bhutan for many years. There, doctors and traditional healers come together regularly, for team meetings. Together they think about how they can assist the patient in the best way in their recovery process. They consult, and hand over cases when their own treatment method reaches its limits, and no longer helps the patient.

AFTERCARE OF THE DECEASED

I would like to take this opportunity to pay attention to a field that is not considered by many people and should be an integral part of terminal care, in my opinion: the after-care and support of people who have already died.

Life continues after death. This is proven, among other evidence, by reports of near-death-experiences of countless people. In many spiritual traditions, it is said that people also need to be supported on their journey in the beyond worlds and the between worlds, after their transition. For example, Tibetan monks accompany a deceased person for several weeks after their passage, through prayers and mantras. These help the deceased to find their way in the spiritual world and to master the dangers that are lurking there.

Spiritual traditions say that, especially people who have not walked on the spiritual path in their lifetime need help in their transition process. There is a greater danger for them to get stuck on certain levels, in the beyond worlds. I do not want to deepen this topic at this point. There is a lot of literature about it. But at this point, I would like to draw attention to the great importance of this topic. Currently, countless souls hang in the intermediate worlds and need the help of sensitive and empathetic people, who have a correspondence, task, and ability for this work in their soul plan.

Chapter 6
Conclusion

We, as humanity, stand at a crossroads and are called to create a change together. The change of the situation on Earth must happen «Now». We cannot wait anymore. The three-day cleansing process will come as a necessary step for the healing of the earth. We all will be affected by it. If it comes today or tomorrow plays an important role because today we can influence and change the situation in our favor. The opportunity window is open «Now».

If we let pass the opportunity that is given to us pass, the consequences for us humans, individually as well as collectively, will be connected with facing greater challenges. I cannot make the seriousness and urgency of the current situation clear enough and recommend that everyone take this warning seriously.

At the present time, we are all called to overcome all paralysing fears and to work with courage and creativity for constructive solutions. Giving the highest priority to the saving of the earth should be our most important thing in this current time. If we save the earth, we save ourselves.

If many people would share this as a priority, in many parts of the world, we can make a major change within a short time.

Decide to become a citizen of the new age! Say resolutely «No» to egoism and negativity and «Yes» to love, to the earth, to the soul, to God, and to peace. Think about how you can actively shape the change and implement your ideas. Everyone counts and is needed!

Despite all the challenges, it is important to remember that we live in an incredibly blissful time. Within a short period of time, we are able to go through major developmental processes that normally require several lives in other periods of history.

Do not let this precious time pass! Focus on your inner development, especially in this current time, and use every valuable day!

From the point of view of the divine, we have all the support we need, for all these processes, so that we can succeed.

To be able to accept this help, we are called upon to transform our human arrogance into humility and to acknowledge that we can no longer solve many problems of the current time without help. To be able to help us, the bright spiritual world needs our trust and our willingness to cooperate with its knowledge and wisdom.

Let us accept this offer and take advantage of these opportunities!

**«May this book inspire you,
to be a part of the change!»**

Bibliography

Books

- **Berndt, Stefan** (2015). Alois Irlmaier. Ein Mann sagt, was er sieht. Der Seher - Die Prophezeiungen - Neuste Recherchen. Regensburg: Reichel Verlag, fourth edition.
- **Caddy, Renata** (2013). Segen von Babaji. Begegnung mit dem Meister vom Himalaya. Darmstadt: Tschirner Verlag, first edition.
- **Megre, Wladmir** (2013). Anastasia. Tochter der Taiga. Jestetten: Govinda-Verlag, ninth edition.
- **Reichel, Gertraud** (1996). Babaji spricht: Prophezeiungen und Lehren. Regensburg: Reichel Verlag, third edition.
- **Stern, Rose** (2015). Der Prophet des Neuen Äons. Nostradamus. Die göttliche Weissagung Jetzt!. Flörsbachtal: Klecks-Verlag, first edition.
- **Walsch, Neale Donald** (2006). Gespräche mit Gott. Ein ungewöhnlicher Dialog Bd. 1. München: Goldman Verlag, fourth edition.

Online-Newspaper articles

- **Ehrenstein, Claudia** (2014). «Deutsche schlachten pro Jahr 750 Millionen Tiere», in: Die Welt, 01/ 2014 [Online newspaper article], available under: http://www.welt.de/politik/deutschland/article12370032 9/Deutsche-schlachten-pro-Jahr-750-Millionen-Tiere.html, published on: 09.01.2014, [Last viewed on 06.08.2016, 22:43].

- **Focus Online** (Autor o. A.) (2012). «15.000 Liter Wasser für ein Kilo Rindfleisch», in Focus Online 03/ 2012 [Online newspaper article], available under http://www.focus.de/wissen/mensch/umwelt-weltwassertag-wassersparen-bei nahrungsproduktion_aid_726582.html, published on 22.03.2012, [Last viewed on 06.08.2016, 16:21].
- **Göring, Olaf** (1995), «Die Erde verliert ihren kosmischen Schutzmantel», in: Die Welt, 12/1995 [Online newspaper article], available under: http://www.welt.de/print-welt/article665243/Die-Erde-verliert-ihren-kosmischen-Schutzmantel.html, published on: 29.12.1995, [Last viewed on 13.01.2016, 17:22].
- **Merkel, Wolfgang W.** (2010). «Was passiert, wenn das Erdmagnetfeld kollabiert?», in: Die Welt, 08/ 2010 [Online newspaper article], available under: http://www.welt.de/wissenschaft/article9090079/Was-passiert-wenn-das-Erdmagnetfeld-kollabiert.html, published on: 19.08.2010, [Last viewed on 25.01.2016, 15:13].
- **Rotter, David** (2013). «Die Tekos Schule: 11 Jahre Schule in einem Jahr», in: SEIN, 01/2013 [Online newspaper article], available under: https://www.sein.de/die-tekos-schule-11-jahre-schule-in-einem-jahr/, published on: 29.01.2013, [Last viewed on 18.07.2016, 17:58].

- **Spiegel Online** (Author w.s.) (2006). «Alte Logbücher: Erdmagnetfeld schwächelt erst seit kurzem», in: Spiegel Online 05/2006 [Online newspaper article], available under: http://www.spiegel.de/wissenschaft/natur/alte-logbücher-erdmagnetfeld-schwächelt-erst-seit-kurzem-a-415757.html, published on: 12.05.2006, [Last viewed on 13.01.2016, 17:02].

Further Internet sources/ Texts from homepage

- **Bible Gateway** (2010). King James Version. Isaiah chapter 24, 1-20. Available under: https://www.biblegateway.com/passage/?search=Isaiah+24&version=KJV. [online], [Last viewed on 05.01.2018, 21:46].
- **Bible Gateway** (2010). King James Version. Luke chapter 21, 25-35. Available under: https://www.biblegateway.com/passage/?search=Luke+21&version=KJV [online], [Last viewed on 05.01.2018, 21:49].
- **Bible Gateway** (2010). King James Version. Matthew chapter 24, 1-51. Available under: https://www.biblegateway.com/passage/?search=Matthew+24&version=KJV [online], [Last viewed on 05.01.2018, 21:51].
- **Bible Gateway** (2010). King James Version. 2 Timothy 3. Available under: https://www.biblegateway.com/passage/?search=2+Timo

thy+3&version=KJV [online], [Last viewed on 05.01.2018, 21:53].

- **Fleischatlas** (2014). Daten und Fakten über Tiere als Nahrungsmittel. Available under: https://www.bund.net/fileadmin/bundnet/publikationen/landwirschaft/140108_bund_landwirtschaft_fleischatlas_2014.pdf, [online], [Last viewed on 07.08.2016, 21:39].
- **Food and agriculture organization of the United Nation** (2010). Global Forrest Resources Assessment. Main report, No. 163. Available under: http://www.fao.org/docrep/013/i1757e/i1757e.pdf, [online], [Last viewed on 06.08.2016, 23:08].
- **Gutemann, Gerd** (2016). «Prophezeiungen der Hopi-Indianer». Available under: http://www.j-lorber.de/proph/seher/hopis.htm (Processing status: 16.01.2016) [online], [Last viewed on 18.12.2015, 12:16].
- **Pro Regenwald** (o. A.). «Fleisch ist ein Stück Lebenskraft.» Available under: https://www.pro-regenwald.de/hg_fleisch, [online], [Last viewed on 06.08.2016, 23:08].

Films

- **AnotherPeakDoku** (2013), Bhutan: Paradies der Heilpflanzen (arte, 2005) [youtube-Video], published on 21.03.2013. Available under: https://www.youtube.com/watch?v=p9Lxm-kkcWo, [Last viewed on 15.07.2016].

- **Baldus Hain** (2014), Klassische Europäische Prophetie am Beispiel Alois Irlmaiers Alpenparlament [youtube-Video], published on 08.02.2014. Available under: https://www.youtube.com/watch?v=SqRrxPgfZRQ, [Last viewed on 05.12.2015].
- **B-N-D.net** (2011), Magnetischer Wechsel: Die Pole spielen verrückt – Der Polsprung schulwissenschaftlich erklärt [youtube-Video], published on 30.09.2011. Available under: https://www.youtube.com/watch?v=ToI58BKxg7Y, [Last viewed on 29.12.2015].
- **Berndt Klank** (2013), dreitägige Dunkelheit [youtube-Video], published on 16.07.2013. Available under: https://www.youtube.com/watch?v=G1QqVED390k, [Last viewed on 23.11.2015].
- **Consciousness2mind** (2014), Richard Kandlin (17) – Natürliches lernen an der Schetinin Schule (LAIS-Schule) [youtube-Video], published on 22.07.2014. Available under: https://www.youtube.com/watch?v=q-mVMaIYg4k, [Last viewed on 15.07.2016].
- **Cordis ANIMA** (2015), 3 Tage Finsternis • 3 Days of Darkness! [youtube-Video], published on 19.03.2015. Available under: https://www.youtube.com/watch?v=Xgw7d2gaLFg, [Last viewed on 20.01.2016].
- **dazzafact** (2014), Die Prophezeiungen der Bibel – Was kommt auf die Menschheit zu? [youtube-Video], published on 15.01.2014. Available under:

https://www.youtube.com/watch?v=3xFUdtaYVu4, [Last viewed on 28.12.2015].

- **Discover Ministries** (2016), 15-Year-Old Secular Jewish Boy Nathan's Vision of WWIII on Blood Moon: Gog Magog Future of Israel [youtube-Video], published on 08.01.2016. Available under: https://www.youtube.com/watch?v=RZd53ynuyrg, [Last viewed on 05.03.2016].
- **Goger 1978** (2011), Neuzeit Prophet german Deutsch Edgar Cayce [youtube-Video], published on 23.10.2011. Available under: https://www.youtube.com/watch?v=I77Z1G2xnbM, [Last viewed on 07.01.2016].
- **HERNANDERSON** (2008), Don Alejandro - Mayan message to the world -OFFICIAL VIDEO [youtube-Video], published on 15.11.2008. Available under: https://www.youtube.com/watch?v=Dw0HXgt6dcM, [Last viewed on 15.12.2015].
- **Human the movie** (2015), HUMAN Extended version VOL.1, Regisseur Yann Arthus-Bertrand [youtube-Video], published on 11.09.2015. Available under: https://www.youtube.com/watch?v=vdb4XGVTHkE, [Last viewed on 14.12.2015
- **L.O.V.E Production** (2015), Schöpfung – Wie die Anastasía-Bücher die Welt verändern! [youtube-Video], published on 03.05.2015. Available under: https://www.youtube.com/watch?v=KTsYT0bP9qg, [Last viewed on 06.07.2016].

- **Mariensohn** (2012), Prophezeiungen und Warnungen
  [youtube-Video], veröffentlicht am 03.07.2012. Available
  under:
  https://www.youtube.com/watch?v=eHuBF8OHAHQ,
  [Last viewed on 15.01.2016].
- **Mariensohn** (2009), 1A wie alles begann (Vortrag von
  Vassula Ryden) [youtube-Video], published on 05.05.2009.
  Available under:
  https://www.youtube.com/watch?v=uRBjNQs7HgE&list=P
  L007E1B3C4B508394&index=1, [Last viewed on
  15.01.2016].
- **Mariensohn** (2009), 3 C vertraut sein mit Jesus (Vortrag
  von Vassula Ryden) [youtube-Video], published on
  05.05.2009, available under
  https://www.youtube.com/watch?v=uRBjNQs7HgE&list=P
  L007E1B3C4B508394&index=1, [Last viewed on
  15.01.2016].
- **MrChannel** (2014), Garten statt Supermarkt –
  Selbstversorgung aus dem Garten [youtube-Video],
  published on 01.08.2013. Available under:
  https://www.youtube.com/watch?v=8ek-id-Du6M, [Last
  viewed on 06.07.2016].
- **Naturnetzwerk net** (2014), Rodnoje – Familienlandsitze in
  Russland & Das Leben dort – Doku [youtube-Video],
  published on 20.08.2014. Available under:
  https://www.youtube.com/watch?v=rU9DyBr4BX0, [Last
  viewed on 06.07.2016].

- **OrlaFl** (2012), Eine leuchtende Botschaft. Tekos – eine Schule der Zukunft [youtube-Video], published on 13.06.2012. Available under: https://www.youtube.com/watch?v=xLnz_kJXd98, [Last viewed on 15.07.2016].
- **Over Do Za MoZa 1444** (2015), Beste Doku! – New World Order – Bewußtsein auf höherer Ebene [youtube-Video], published on 16.07.2013. Available under: https://www.youtube.com/watch?v=605ln7UZ6_Q&featu re=youtu.be, [Last viewed on 06.07.2016].
- **Pablo Arellano** (2012), Drunvalo Melchizedek – The Pole Shift 2012 – by Pablo Arellano [youtube-Video], published on 14.12.2012. Available under: https://www.youtube.com/watch?v=BiDXGTq-xs0, [Last viewed on.02.2016].
- **Pan AfricanMarkets** (2012), Red Crow: Native American Prophecy [youtube-Video], published on 01.10.2012. Available under: https://www.youtube.com/watch?v=XLLVz0d3gao, [Last viewed on 15.12.2015].
- **Roth Sid** (2015), It´s Supernatural! Guest Rick Renner [Video], published on 09.03.2015. Available under: http://sidroth.org/television/tv-archives/rick-renner, [Last viewed on 01.04.2016].
- **Satsang-ful** (2015), PROPHEZEIUNGEN – Dr. Michael Vogt u Nicki Vogt – Vorhersagen des Alois Irlmaier (8.3.2013 Sendung, Thema: Prophezeiungen und Vorhersagen als Warnung? Alois Irlmaier, vorgestellt durch Prof. Dr.

Michael Vogt und Niki Vogt zu Gast bei Norbert Brakenhagen. TimeToDo.ch.) [youtube-Video], published on 10.03.2013. Available under: https://www.youtube.com/watch?v=wflwy47nGWc, [Last viewed on 23.11.2015].

- **Schatzliste** (2015), Revolution der Permakultur – Miracle Farms, Quebec Kanada | deutsch [youtube-Video], published on 30.06.2015. Available under: https://www.youtube.com/watch?v=GsJgR0ro6oc, [Last viewed on 06.07.2016].
- **Scholé** – Muße für Herz und Geist (2015), Lernmethoden der Schetinin Schule von Richard Kandlin. Teil 1 Vortrag [youtube-Video], published on 14.03.2015. Available under: https://www.youtube.com/watch?v=6FIMsaacx4o, [Last viewed on 15.07.2016].
- **Scholé** – Muße für Herz und Geist (2015), Lernmethoden der Schetinin Schule von Richard Kandlin. Teil 2 Fragen [youtube-Video], published on 14.03.2015. Available under: https://www.youtube.com/watch?v=M-gif-Azo1I, [Last viewed on 15.07.2016].
- **sontttu78** (2013), Ich war fünf Stunden tot – Andreas Berglesow AVC [youtube-Video], published on 29.08.2013. Available under: https://www.youtube.com/watch?v=aQiD6ofLgrE, [Last viewed on 01.04.2016].
- **timetodotv** (2014), TimeToDo.ch 10.02.2014, Hat Nostradamus den Polsprung vorausgesagt [youtube-Video], published on 11.02.2014. Available under:

https://www.youtube.com/watch?v=qz9Lb4SDRdk, [Last viewed on 25.11.2015].

- **התורה אש** (2015), The new film of the 15 -year-old boy who Experienced Clinical Death who saw the wwiii (11 minutes) [youtube-Video], published on 02.12.2015. Available under: https://www.youtube.com/watch?v=fGsiANZmFb8, [Last viewed on 05.03.2016].

List of pictures and graphics

Following pictures and graphics are
©2015 by Stephanie Bunk

- **Bunk, Stephanie** (2014): Stephanie Bunk. Markdorf.
- **Bunk, Stephanie** (2015): The seven positive and negative planes of existence. Stuttgart.
- **Bunk, Stephanie** (2015): The four ages of the universe. Stuttgart.
- **Bunk, Stephanie** (2015): Humanity and nature in Kaliyuga. Markdorf.
- **Bunk, Stephanie** (2015): Humanity and nature in Satyayuga. Markdorf.
- **Bunk, Stephanie** (2015): The three gunas. Using images from www.fotolia.com:
  Photo ID: 2683042, Joemonias
  Photo ID: 1357485, Pezibear
  Photo ID: 1209630, Free-Photos.

Further pictures / Extraneous Copyright

- **Balaji Studio** (2016): Mahanandha Siddha. Bangalore.
- **Balaji Studio** (2016): The temple of Mahadevamalai. Bangalore. Changed by Stephanie Bunk on 01.04.2016.
- **Berndt, Stephan** (2015). Aussagen zu Teilaspekten der Dreitägigen Finsternis, in: Berndt, Stephan (2015). Alois Irlmaier. Ein Mann sagt, was er sieht. Der Seher-Die Prophezeiungen-Neuste Recherchen. Regensburg: Reichel Verlag, 4. Auflage, p.306.
- **NCEI** (2015). Wandering of the geomagnetic poles, [published on o.A.], http://www.ngdc.noaa.gov/geomag/GeomagneticPoles.shtml, [Last viewed on 01.04.2016].

215

EARTH IN BALANCE

WORLD-CHANGING PROJECTS

HARMONY BETWEEN
MAN AND NATURE

Be the change!
Together. Humanly. Lovingly. Changing.

Imagine, many people all over the world unite, united in the dream to create a world of humanity, love, joy, peace, and harmony for all human beings and creatures. Imagine you are a part of this movement and would allow yourself to realize and manifest your dream for a better world. And imagine you would be supported by a growing and wonderful community that inspire each other, believe in you with your dream, and supports you with everything you need, to make that dream become true.

Deeply inspired by this vision, in May 2017, Earth in balance was founded. Earth in balance is a movement that supports everyone who is ready for a change, and to manifest their dreams and wishes for a better world in the form of small and large projects. Because when many people in many places do good things, they can change the face of the world.

We are looking for people in all cities and places all over the world who want to grow beyond themselves, who have the courage, love, and spirit to say «goodbye» to the old structures and to create a healthy world in balance and harmony.

www.earth-in-balance.org

Find inner peace and harmony!
Initiation in Maha Poorna Atma Yoga

«Maha Poorna Atma Yoga» means «Great Purification of the Soul». It is a simple practice that works from the highest frequency level of nature, to help to purify the subconscious mind of conditioning and destructive responses and emotions. These include fear, guilt, greed, shame, anger, jealousy, envy. These subconscious impressions are also called «Samskaras» in Sanskrit. They obscure the luminous consciousness and are one of the main reasons why we repeatedly fall out of our equilibrium and block our inner growth process. Through the practice of Maha Poorna Atma Yoga, the energetic charge on destructive reaction patterns is getting gradually transformed. This makes it easier to dismantle them. In this way, it becomes possible for man to develop inner peace, to come into a state of equilibrium, and to build harmonious ways, by reacting from the soul-level.

Maha Poorna Atma Yoga also fulfills another important function. It is not only a cleanser for your own soul, but also for the collective. It reduces negative energy fields in the collective consciousness.

www.maha-poorna-atma-yoga.org

217

Healing and Transforming the Energy World!

The company NEW ENERGY WORLD (NEW) has been commissioned by nature to help humanity to heal nature, to correct errors and to raise the energy frequency on Earth to the level of the golden age. For this, alchemical recipes were transmitted from the spiritual world through the palm leaf library by the master and seer Agastya Rishi. The more these remedies spread throughout the earth, the more the energetic equilibrium of the earth will be stabilized. Their effects come from the highest frequency level in nature. They are unique and cannot be copied. The recipes work 100% in harmony with nature and do not produce secondary frequencies (comparable to side effects). To be able to spread the remedies, they will be incorporated into everyday products. NEW combines the effects of the alchemical formulas with modern product design and ecological commitment.

www.new-energy-world.org